MySQL Management and Administration with Navicat

Master the tools you thought you knew and discover the features you never knew existed

Gökhan Ozar

BIRMINGHAM - MUMBAI

MySQL Management and Administration with Navicat

Copyright © 2012 Packt Publishing

First published: September 2012

Production Reference: 1060912

Published by Packt Publishing Ltd.
Livery Place
35 Livery Street
Birmingham B3 2PB, UK.

ISBN 9781849687-46-1

www.packtpub.com

Cover Image by Artie Ng (artherng@yahoo.com.au)

Credits

Author
Gökhan Ozar

Reviewers
Nick Au

Matthew Yau

Acquisition Editor
Alex Newbury

Lead Technical Editor
Alex Newbury

Technical Editor
Kaustubh S. Mayekar

Copy Editor
Insiya Morbiwala

Project Coordinator
Abhishek Kori

Proofreader
Maria Gould

Indexer
Monica Ajmera Mehta

Production Coordinator
Nitesh Thakur

Cover Work
Nitesh Thakur

About the Author

Gökhan Ozar is an IT professional with both hands-on and outsourcing expertise in the areas of application development, database design, data analysis, project management, systems integration, training, support, and delegation of support.

A graduate in 1999 of Bilkent University in Ankara, Turkey, he started his career as a Web Designer and Developer, making database-driven web applications on a variety of platforms.

During his high school years at the age of 16, he was known within the Mac user communities in Turkey as the maker of an adventure game called The Journey, made exclusively for older Macs running on Mac OS versions prior to OS X.

He has had experience in various domains of IT, such as business intelligence, data warehousing, and quality assurance, besides software development mainly on Java EE and .NET platforms. He went on to build his career working with the Business Process Management/Electronic Document Workflow software.

He also runs several blogs, which are accessible from his personal website at `http://gokhan.ozar.net`, and also welcomes new followers on Twitter (`twitter.com/skyhan`).

About the Reviewers

Nick Au, who graduated from the Hong Kong University of Science and Technology, has been working as a Software Developer at PremiumSoft for over 10 years. Now he is the lead developer for the Windows version of Navicat, leading a team of over 10 programmers.

Matthew Yau joined PremiumSoft after he graduated from the Hong Kong Polytechnic University in 2000. After taking up a position in web programming for the first 2 years, he has focused on developing the Navicat series since 2002. Now, he is working at the managerial level for the development of Navicat and other softwares for the Company.

www.PacktPub.com

Support files, eBooks, discount offers, and more

You might want to visit www.PacktPub.com for support files and downloads related to your book.

Did you know that Packt offers eBook versions of every book published, with PDF and ePub files available? You can upgrade to the eBook version at www.PacktPub.com and as a print book customer, you are entitled to a discount on the eBook copy. Get in touch with us at service@packtpub.com for more details.

At www.PacktPub.com, you can also read a collection of free technical articles, sign up for a range of free newsletters and receive exclusive discounts and offers on Packt books and eBooks.

http://PacktLib.PacktPub.com

Do you need instant solutions to your IT questions? PacktLib is Packt's online digital book library. Here, you can access, read and search across Packt's entire library of books.

Why Subscribe?

- Fully searchable across every book published by Packt
- Copy and paste, print, and bookmark content
- On demand and accessible via web browser

Free Access for Packt account holders

If you have an account with Packt at www.PacktPub.com, you can use this to access PacktLib today and view nine entirely free books. Simply use your login credentials for immediate access.

Instant Updates on New Packt Books

Get notified! Find out when new books are published by following @PacktEnterprise on Twitter, or the *Packt Enterprise* Facebook page.

Table of Contents

Preface

Navicat is a GUI tool used for managing every aspect of a MySQL Server, such as managing visual tools as well as an intelligent code editor for handcoding SQL and stored procedures. While some of its features are fairly intuitive, some of them require guidance to be discovered and learned.

The book starts with creating basic server connection setups, designing databases from scratch, or importing existing data. Then it continues with using advanced features, such as designing functions and stored procedures, creating event triggers, and creating and scheduling batch jobs.

The chapters are ordered in a logical progression, where the user starts from simple structures to complex design, and is gradually introduced to advanced features. By the end of the last chapter, the reader should be able to handle every aspect of database administration as well as how to master the intelligent code editor, in the case of a development need, such as functions and procedures.

For intermediate and advanced level MySQL users and administrators, the book could be used as a reference guide, and chapters need not be followed in any order.

What this book covers

Chapter 1, Getting Started, gives an introduction to the Navicat Database Administration tool with a GUI and describes how to set up different kinds of connections, from basic settings to advanced configurations.

Chapter 2, Working with Databases, discusses the fundamentals of working with database objects, such as tables, views, functions, and events, along with designing queries using Navicat's visual tools.

Chapter 3, Data Management with Navicat, takes you through the process of data management. The topics covered are import and export of data in a variety of formats, direct data transfer between different databases, data and structure synchronization, backup/restore operations, and creating and scheduling of batch jobs.

Chapter 4, Data Modeling with Navicat, guides you through the steps involved in visual data modeling, so as to help us learn how to design data models using GUI tools; create, edit, and manipulate table structures from within the visual editor; forward-engineer a data model into a .sql file; and reverse-engineer an existing database into visual representations.

Chapter 5, Database Maintenance and Security Management, discusses the essentials of basic DBA functions regarding the security and maintenance of MySQL using Navicat. It walks you through the necessary steps to create and edit MySQL users, manage the access privileges, and perform maintenance tasks, such as database analysis, optimization, and repairs.

Chapter 6, Designing Reports with Navicat, discusses report design and provides instructions on the various steps involved in conceiving, creating, and customizing reports based on your MySQL database objects.

Appendix, Additional Tips and Tricks, provides some additional tips and tricks to make the most of Navicat, with guided instructions on how to copy your settings to another Navicat user or computer, monitor the MySQL server, intervene the running processes, power search databases, and discover a new way of designing queries.

What you need for this book

To run the examples in the book, the following software will be required:

- MySQL server (Mac/Win/Linux):
    - ◦ MySQL Server 5.1 or later
- Navicat (Mac/Win/Linux):
    - ◦ Navicat Premium or Navicat for MySQL 9.0 or later (*Chapter 4, Data Modeling with Navicat* and *Chapter 5, Database Maintenance and Security Management* require Navicat 10 or later)
    - ◦ Designing Reports (*Chapter 6, Designing Reports with Navicat*) requires Navicat for Windows

Who this book is for

This book is especially for:

- Database administrators/DBAs (both novice and expert)
- Developers who use MySQL as a backend database (both novice and expert)
- IT Analysts (both novice and expert)

Non-IT people who just want to extract sensible data from a MySQL database (both novice and expert), and people who need to have at least some basic knowledge of databases in a client/server architecture will find this book useful.

Beginners can learn from scratch the fundamentals of database design and administration (and even some development), especially, thanks to the tutorials featured in this book.

Experts can unlock certain mysteries of Navicat, which consist of useful, but seemingly hidden or unobvious features.

Conventions

In this book, you will find a number of styles of text that distinguish between different kinds of information. Here are some examples of these styles, and an explanation of their meaning.

Code words in text are shown as follows: "If you're using a Mac, Navicat should simply be in your `Applications` folder unless you dragged and dropped it elsewhere from the installer window."

A block of code is set as follows:

```
BEGIN
    INSERT INTO emp_log SET emp_id = NEW.id, date_created = NOW();
END
```

Any command-line input or output is written as follows:

```
CREATE TABLE if not exists emp_log (
  id int auto_increment primary key,
  emp_id int,
  date_created datetime
  );
```

New terms and **important words** are shown in bold. Words that you see on the screen, in menus or dialog boxes for example, appear in the text like this: "To launch Navicat in Windows 7 and earlier, go to **Start menu** | **All Programs** | **PremiumSoft** and click on the version of Navicat you have installed on your PC."

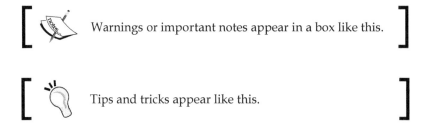

Warnings or important notes appear in a box like this.

Tips and tricks appear like this.

Reader feedback

Feedback from our readers is always welcome. Let us know what you think about this book—what you liked or may have disliked. Reader feedback is important for us to develop titles that you really get the most out of.

To send us general feedback, simply send an e-mail to `feedback@packtpub.com`, and mention the book title through the subject of your message.

If there is a topic that you have expertise in and you are interested in either writing or contributing to a book, see our author guide on `www.packtpub.com/authors`.

Customer support

Now that you are the proud owner of a Packt book, we have a number of things to help you to get the most from your purchase.

Errata

Although we have taken every care to ensure the accuracy of our content, mistakes do happen. If you find a mistake in one of our books—maybe a mistake in the text or the code—we would be grateful if you would report this to us. By doing so, you can save other readers from frustration and help us improve subsequent versions of this book. If you find any errata, please report them by visiting `http://www.packtpub.com/support`, selecting your book, clicking on the **errata submission form** link, and entering the details of your errata. Once your errata are verified, your submission will be accepted and the errata will be uploaded to our website, or added to any list of existing errata, under the Errata section of that title.

Piracy

Piracy of copyright material on the Internet is an ongoing problem across all media. At Packt, we take the protection of our copyright and licenses very seriously. If you come across any illegal copies of our works, in any form, on the Internet, please provide us with the location address or website name immediately so that we can pursue a remedy.

Please contact us at `copyright@packtpub.com` with a link to the suspected pirated material.

We appreciate your help in protecting our authors, and our ability to bring you valuable content.

Questions

You can contact us at `questions@packtpub.com` if you are having a problem with any aspect of the book, and we will do our best to address it.

1
Getting Started

This chapter is intended as an introduction to the Navicat Database Administration tool with a **graphical user interface (GUI)**, and describes how to set up different kinds of connections and basic settings to advanced configurations, such as SSH, to an installed MySQL server. In this chapter, you will learn about the following:

- Different editions of Navicat, which is good for what and for whom
- Setting up a basic connection to a MySQL server
- Setting up advanced connections, such as SSH or HTTP tunneling

Enter Navicat

Navicat is not only a powerful, sophisticated, and easy-to-use database administration tool with a GUI , but also a very useful aide for developers who work on database-driven applications. It is available for Windows, Mac, and Linux.

Navicat for MySQL is the first member of the Navicat family with advanced features allowing you to import/export data, back up, or transfer an entire database to another server and design queries in a GUI with point-and-click and drag-and-drop features.

Navicat Premium is the ultimate member of the family, an all-in-one database administration, and migration tool combining all Navicat versions enabling the user to connect to MySQL, SQL Server, SQLite, Oracle, and PostgreSQL databases simultaneously within a single application, making database administration of multiple brands of databases substantially easier.

While databases other than MySQL are outside the scope of this book, you may want to check out other titles from Packt, such as those on Oracle database (www.packtpub.com/books/oracle-database) and Microsoft SQL Server (www.packtpub.com/books/microsoft-sql-server).

Navicat is not a free product, but you can easily obtain a 30-day evaluation from the website of PremiumSoft, the company that created the product and brought it to the market.

Throughout the book, the examples will be shown using Navicat Premium version 10.0.9, although you can follow every example and exercise using Navicat for MySQL 10.0.9. Even if you have a version of Navicat as old as v.8.0, you should be able to keep up with the book for most of the examples.

To download Navicat, you can go to www.navicat.com/download/download.html and get either Navicat for MySQL or Navicat Premium. The most up-to-date version was 10.0.9 at the time of this writing.

Setting up a connection to the database

At this point, I assume you already have your MySQL server installed, set up, and running as well as Navicat, so that we can get our hands dirty with Navicat right away.

To launch Navicat in Windows 7 and earlier, go to **Start menu** | **All Programs** | **PremiumSoft** and click on the version of Navicat you have installed on your PC.

If you're using a Mac, Navicat should simply be in your Applications folder unless you dragged and dropped it elsewhere from the installer window.

In order to define a new connection, go to the **File** menu or the **Connection** button, which is the first icon in the Navicat's main toolbar (or ribbon, as we might call it) and select **File** | **New Connection** | **MySQL** to open up the connection profile window titled **MySQL - New Connection**, where we can specify the settings for the connection we want to establish.

You can refer to the following screenshot:

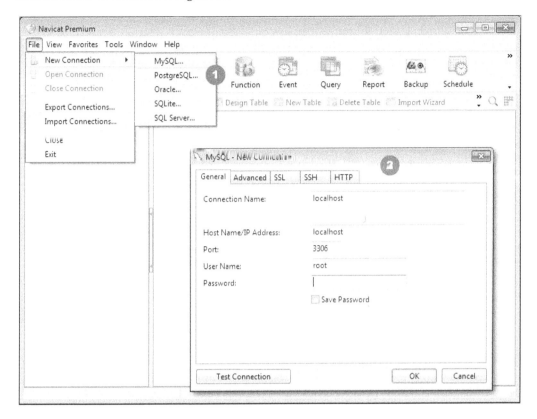

As you can see in the second part of the screenshot, the **MySQL - New Connection** window is where you can specify the settings to define a connection. It has five tabs; the first of which is where you set the basic connection properties and it is sufficient in most cases, which are as follows:

- **Connection Name**: It is totally up to you, so you can enter any name to describe your connection.

- **Host Name/IP Address**: It is exceedingly intuitive, where you can either enter the domain name of your database server or its IP address.

- **Port**: This field includes the TCP/IP port number of the MySQL server which in most cases is 3306.

- **User Name**: This field includes the database username (I'm going with `root` here which is the default admin user for my newly installed local server).

- **Password**: This field includes password for the above entered username. In fresh MySQL installations, `root` comes with a blank password, so if this is your first time connecting to the database server you just installed, you might want to leave this blank at this time as I will guide you how to modify all these settings at the end of the chapter.

If you are connecting to a remote MySQL server, you must make sure that remote access privileges are granted for the username you will be using. In some cases where the MySQL service provider does not provide direct access to the server remotely, connecting via **Secure Shell** (**SSH**) or an HTTP tunnel might be an alternative solution. We'll see how to set up these kinds of connections respectively in the following sections.

Connecting via Secure Shell (SSH)

SSH is a command line tool to log into a server or another computer over a network in a secure manner to run commands on the remote machine or to transfer data. For increased security, SSH provides a strong authentication mechanism either by using a password or a public/private key pair also known simply as a public key.

In order to set up your connection to the MySQL server via SSH, first enter the basic connection settings as described in the previous section, then go to the **SSH** tab in the connection settings window, click on the checkbox labeled **Use SSH Tunnel**, and then enter the following information:

- **Host Name/IP Address**: This field includes the address or the IP of the SSH server.

- **Port**: This field includes the port number of the SSH server (the default is 22).

- **User Name**: This field includes the user of the SSH server, which is usually a UNIX machine and not a username of the database.

- **Authentication method**: This field allows you to choose between **Password** authentication and **Public Key** authentication, whichever's applicable.

- **Password** (if applicable): This field includes the password of the SSH user (not the database).

- **Private Key** (if applicable): This field appears if you choose the **Public Key** authentication, in which you need to specify the path to your private key file by clicking on the small rectangular button proceeding it.

- **Passphrase** (if applicable): This field also shows up in the case of **Public key** authentication and is used in conjunction with the **Private Key**. It's basically like a password, but it applies to your key and not an account.

Connecting via an HTTP tunnel

In some cases, it is not possible to connect to a server through any protocol but HTTP, especially when one party is behind a firewall. Some companies, for example, want to limit the Internet access of its users so that they are only able to browse the web, and do nothing else; no FTP, no instant messaging, and so on. This is where the HTTP tunneling comes in handy. It allows you to connect to a server (in this case MySQL) through the port 80 (the HTTP default) instead of 3306 or any other port.

To set up an HTTP connection, go through the following steps:

1. Upload the HTTP tunneling script which came with the Navicat installer to the web server where the MySQL server is located. It's a file called `ntunnel_mysql.php`.

2. Go to the tab named **HTTP** in the **MySQL - New Connection** window of Navicat.

3. Enable the checkbox **Use HTTP Tunnel**.

4. Enter the URL of the tunneling script where you uploaded it (for example, `http://www.ozar.net/mysql/ntunnel_mysql.php`).

5. You can check the **Encode outgoing query with base64** option if you know that the web server you uploaded the script has ModSecurity installed.

6. If the tunneling script is on a password protected server or your internet connection is over a proxy, you can provide the required authentication details under the **Authentication** or **Proxy** tab.

 Please note that HTTP tunneling tab and SSH tunneling tab cannot be used at the same time. You need to choose one or the other.

Setting up Secure Sockets Layer (SSL)

Secure Socket Layer (SSL) is a security protocol for establishing an encrypted link between a server and its clients, which ensures the privacy and integrity of all data transmission between the two parties.

To use SSL in Navicat, you need to have an SSL certificate; you can obtain a free solution such as OpenSSL from `www.openssl.org` and install it on your local server, and configure your MySQL server for SSL and set up the server-side certificate for it. Finally, you can set up the client certificate, which you will then be able to obtain from your SSL server. Complete instructions on how to install and set up OpenSSL for MySQL and the certificate for Navicat is explained in the Navicat manual.

Advanced settings

Navicat provides an option for setting advanced database properties which you can control by clicking on the **Advanced** tab in the **MySQL - New Connection** window.

The first field labeled, **Setting Save Path,** allows you to save your settings at a location of your local drive, which you specify. You can tweak some other settings, such as overriding the character encoding, pinging intervals to the database server, auto-connections, using sockets file, that is, `mysql.sock`, and so on.

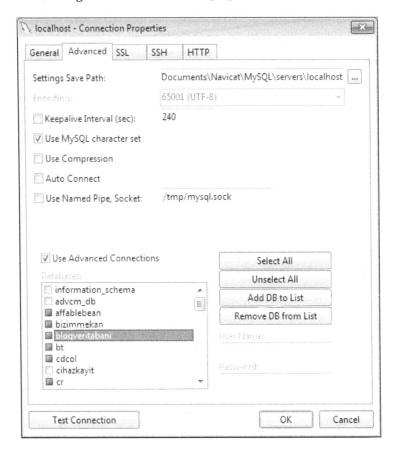

The most useful feature here is the ability to hide and show certain databases on the left pane of Navicat's main window where all your connection profiles and databases that belong to them are listed in a tree view. This feature is activated as soon as you check the **Use advanced connections** checkbox.

The list box titled **Databases** becomes active and every item in the list has a slightly smaller checkbox next to it. The databases whose checkboxes you highlight will be the ones that will appear next time you open the connection. You can also individually specify a username and password for each database. This is especially useful if you have more than one account with different privileges for a given database.

You can also add or remove items to the list by using the buttons on the right-hand side.

Testing and saving your settings

Now that we're done configuring the connection, all we need to do is to test the connection and click on **OK**. We can modify these settings at any time by right- clicking on the name of connection profile listed on the left pane and selecting **Connection Properties...** to bring back our connection profile window.

Summary

In this chapter, we have laid the groundwork for the rest of the book, by learning how to set up connections from within Navicat to a MySQL server in a variety of ways—from using simple customary parameters to secure configurations, such as SSH or HTTP tunneling to overcome limited Internet access situations.

In the next chapter, we will start working with databases, and I will guide you step-by-step in dealing with database objects, such as tables, views, functions, procedures, and designing queries using Navicat's sophisticated yet easy-to-use and addictive tools. The fun is just beginning.

2
Working with Databases

In the previous chapter, we saw how to set up different types of connections to a MySQL server from Navicat. Now that we're ready to get connected to a server, it's time to work with databases. In this chapter you'll learn how to:

- Create a database from scratch
- Create tables and views using Navicat's visual design tools
- Create foreign key constraints and triggers
- Define stored procedures and functions
- Create scheduled events
- Work with database queries

Managing database objects with Navicat

What do we mean by database objects? Basically tables, views, functions, and events are what we refer to as objects. For each of them, there is a toolbar icon in Navicat's main window and they also appear on the tree view list on the left-hand side of the navigation pane. It's possible to hide the object hierarchy from **Tools | Options** by unchecking the **Show objects in connection tree** option, but this would probably be trivial, especially for novice users.

The toolbar in Navicat's main window has large buttons with icons for working with the database objects. Clicking on the **Table** button on the toolbar, for example, is the equivalent of selecting **Tables** in the tree view in the navigation pane titled **Connections**. The larger remaining portion on the right-hand side of the main window, under the toolbar, is called the object pane, which displays the objects of the selected type. The following screenshot shows the objects of **Tables**:

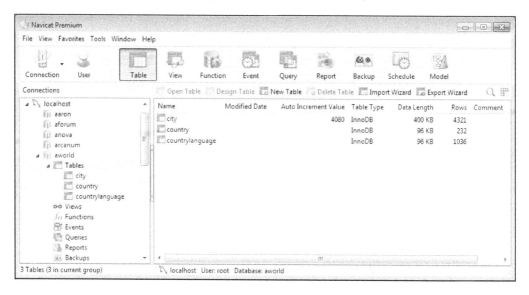

Creating a database from scratch

Navicat makes it extremely easy to create databases and objects, such as tables and views from scratch. As we have established a connection to a MySQL server in the previous chapter, it's time to get started with a blank database of our own. The following steps describe how to create a database from scratch:

1. Double-click on **localhost** (or whatever you named your server) in the **Connections** pane to get connected.

2. Then right-click on the server name, and select **New Database...** from the contextual menu that pops up.

3. In the new smaller window that opens, enter the **Database Name** as `our_first_db`, specify the **Character set** as **utf8--UTF-8 Unicode**, and the **Collation** as **utf8_unicode_ci**.

4. Finally click on **OK**.

Now **our_first_db** should appear among the other databases under **localhost**. By right-clicking on it, you can see what actions you can perform on our new blank database from the contextual pop-up menu, such as opening it, viewing, and editing its properties like **Character set**, **Collation**, and deleting it. There's also an item named **Data Transfer...**in the same pop-up menu, which in my opinion is one of the most powerful features of Navicat. It allows you to transfer data directly to and from another database, which we will cover in *Chapter 3, Data Management with Navicat*.

Due to limitations of MySQL 5.x, it is not possible to rename a database via GUI tools. The best way to do this is to dump the database to an SQL file, create a new database with the desired name, and execute the dump file to fill it with the contents of the previous database. You will also find details of such tasks in *Chapter 3, Data Management with Navicat*.

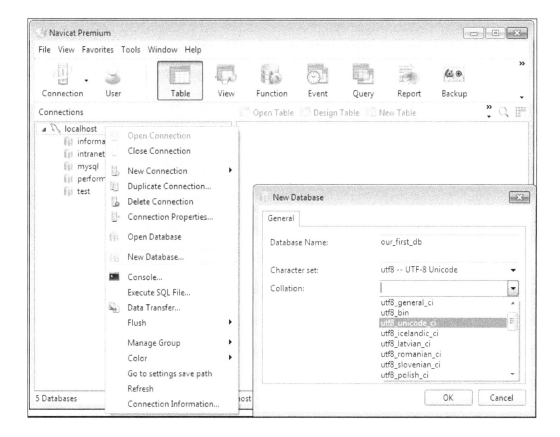

Creating tables

Now let's create some tables for **our_first_db** by following these steps:

1. Select and open the database from the navigation pane by double-clicking on its name.

2. Then either click on the **New Table** button on the toolbar or right-click on **Tables** right under **our_first_db**.

3. Finally, select **New Table** from the pop-up menu.

Navicat's table designer window will appear. The controls here are pretty intuitive. We'll create a department table for a simple employee database and we need three fields for it: id (**int**), name (**varchar**), and manager_id (**int**). To create the fields, follow these steps:

1. Create the first field named id, select **Type** as **int**, leave the **Length** column blank as it will automatically be set to 11, uncheck **Allow Null**, make it a **Primary key** either by clicking on the tiny button with a yellow key icon or by clicking on the empty cell next to the checkbox under **Allow Null**, and then finally check the **Auto Increment** option at the bottom.

2. Adding a new field is as easy as clicking on the **Add Field** button on the toolbar, or pressing the *Tab* key while in the last cell of the most recently created field.

3. Next, we will create the field called name, select **Type** as **varchar**, with 31 characters of length, again uncheck the **Allow Null** checkbox.

4. Finally, select **Type** as **int**, leave the **Length** column blank as it will be automatically be set to 11, and we also want to leave **Allow Null** checked for this one.

5. Now, save this table as department by clicking on one of the **Save** or **Save As** buttons on the toolbar. Navicat also prompts us to save our progress if we just try to close the window without saving anyway. Refer to the following screenshot:

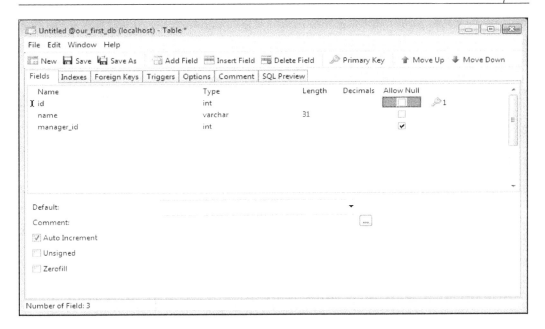

It is possible to interpose a newly-created field between previously created ones by clicking on the existing field and clicking on the **Insert Field** button on the toolbar. We can also change the order of the fields by selecting a field and using the buttons **Move Up** and **Move Down** on the toolbar as we please.

Now we'll repeat the previous steps to create the employee table, but this time defining the fields with the following specifications. In the following table, false implies uncheck and true implies check:

Name	Type	Length	Decimals	Allow Null	Primary Key
id	int			false	X (auto-incrementing)
first_name	varchar	50		true	
last_name	varchar	40		false	
email	varchar	60		true	
title	varchar	35		true	
salary	decimal	10	2	true	
perks	int			false	
department_id	int			true	
manager_id	int			true	

Next, we need to establish some relationships between the two tables by defining some foreign key constraints.

Defining foreign keys

First of all, I recommend saving the table and naming it `employee` (If you happen to close the table designer after that, right-click on the name of the table and choose **Design Table** from the pop-up menu.) While back in the table designer, perform the following steps:

1. Switch to the **Foreign Keys** tab.

2. Enter `fk_employee_4_department` as the name of the foreign key in the first field of the first row.

3. Choose **department_id** for the **Fields** in the second column.

4. Select **our_first_db** as the **Reference Database** in the third column.

5. Pick the **department** table for the **Reference Table** in the fourth column.

6. Select **id** for **Reference Fields**.

7. Optionally, you could specify the cascading options **On Delete** and **On Update** depending on your programming strategy.

   For example, selecting the cascading option **On Delete** in this case means, when a department record is deleted, all employees in that department will also be deleted. Leaving **On Delete** and **On Update** blank will set them to restrict as default, which would mean that you can't delete a department that has employees associated with it.

The above definition will be enforcing a referential integrity check for every employee to be assigned to an existing department via the **department_id** column. It means you can't set a non-existent department ID for a given employee.

Now repeat the steps mentioned earlier to define a foreign key for the **manager_id**, name it `fk_employee_4_manager_id`, set the **Referenced Table** to **employee**, and the **Referenced Fields** to **id**, as shown in the following screenshot:

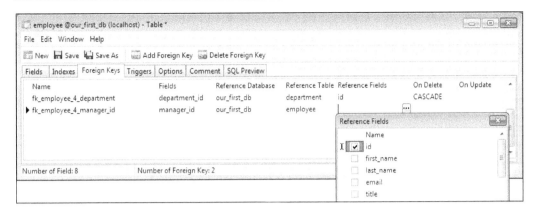

If you switch to the **SQL Preview** tab before saving your changes, you will be able to see a couple of automatically generated SQL commands for adding the designed foreign key constraint(s) to your table. In fact, every change you make on a table's design has corresponding SQL commands, which Navicat performs behind the scenes and executes them on the database server. This can also be useful for learning SQL, or in the case of a server error, for analyzing what went wrong at the backstage. The screenshot of the **SQL Preview** tab is as follows:

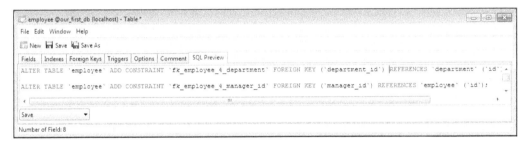

Repeat the same steps for defining a foreign key constraint for the **manager_id** in the **department** table referencing the **id** field of the **employee table**, and name it `fk_department_4_manager`.

As for the table naming convention, I encourage the use of single nouns for table names particularly to make life easier for developers, who use **object-relational mapping** (ORM) APIs that have reverse-engineering tools for the development of database-driven applications.

Navicat's Table Designer also features a tab called **Indexes** that makes creating indexes as easy as creating fields and defining foreign keys using similar methods. In fact, creating a foreign key requires a corresponding index also to be created, and Navicat does that automatically for us by creating an index for every foreign key we define and create.

You will also notice the **Triggers** tab, where you can easily define a trigger for a table. Let's define a simple trigger, which will be activated every time a new row is added to the employee table. For this example, we will need an auxiliary table that I will call **emp_log**.

Defining triggers

You can either practice what you have learned in this section by creating the **emp_log** table using the table designer, by defining three basic fields: id (**Type-int,** check primary key auto-incrementing), emp_id (**Type-int**), and date_created (**Type-datetime**) or by going to the menu bar in Navicat's main window, choosing **Tools | Console...** (alternatively press *F6* as a shortcut) and entering the following command in the MySQL console window:

```
CREATE TABLE if not exists emp_log (
  id int auto_increment primary key,
  emp_id int,
  date_created datetime
);
```

Once the **emp_log** table is created, we're ready to define a trigger that will log every employee record we created in the **employee** table. Right-click on the **employee** table, select **Design Table,** and then perform the following steps in the table designer for the employee table:

1. Go to the **Triggers** tab and click on **Add Trigger** from the toolbar.
2. Name the trigger as ins_trig.
3. In the **Fires** column, select **After**.
4. Check **Insert** and leave the other checkboxes alone.

5. Enter the following code in the **Definition** pane:

```
BEGIN
    INSERT INTO emp_log SET emp_id = NEW.id, date_created = NOW();
END
```

The screenshot of the **Triggers** tab is as follows:

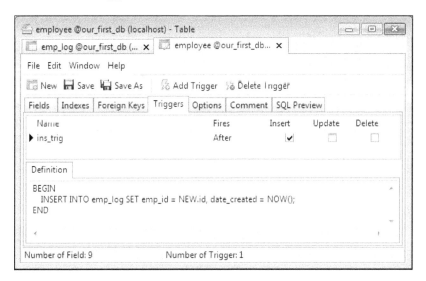

The **Options** tab is another useful aide, which lets you modify certain settings of a MySQL table. A major pitfall for MySQL database designers is that when creating a MySQL table, they might accidentally end up with a MyISAM table, whereas they actually intended to use the InnoDB engine. Navicat makes it easy to change the engine to InnoDB. This kind of modification is not foolproof though. Due to MySQL's internal mechanism, if there's already some data entered in the table, this might make the conversion difficult, and sometimes even impossible. The other options here include **Character set** and **Collation** modification, setting or resetting the **Auto Increment** value for the next record, and maintaining a live checksum for all rows—a feature exclusive to MyISAM tables.

More advanced tweaks are possible on this screen, which is covered in detail in Navicat's manual.

It is also possible to duplicate tables by just clicking on the table's name and selecting **Duplicate Table** from the pop-up menu. Another related cool feature of Navicat is that you can copy a table in the same way and paste it to another database.

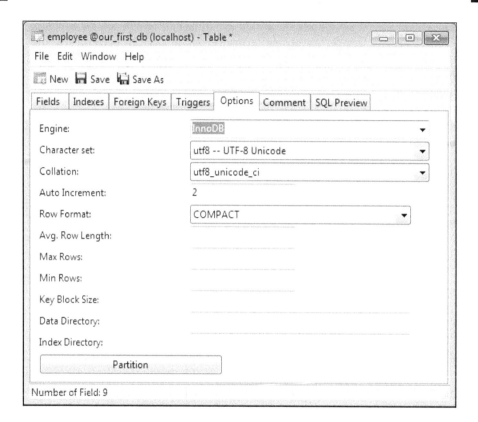

Entering data in tables

Now that we have built the basis for our database, we'd better enter some data in our tables. To open a table for data entry, simply double-click on it.

Navicat provides two ways of data entry in tables: one of them is using the **Grid View**, which is predictably the most common way of entering data just like you would do in a spreadsheet.

Just click on a cell to start entering the data, and when you're done with it, you can press the *Tab* key to move on to the next cell or click on anywhere outside the active cell. Fields with foreign key constraints will contain a small square button for selecting data from a drop-down list, which will present data items from the field of the table to which it has reference(s). In our case, the **department_id** can be selected from the IDs of records entered in the department table as you can see in the following screenshot.

When you're finished with editing the row, you can click on the tiny tick ✓ button at the bottom of the window to save your changes, or the × button to discard them. Click on the (+) plus or minus (-) sign to delete a record if you need to, as shown in the following screenshot:

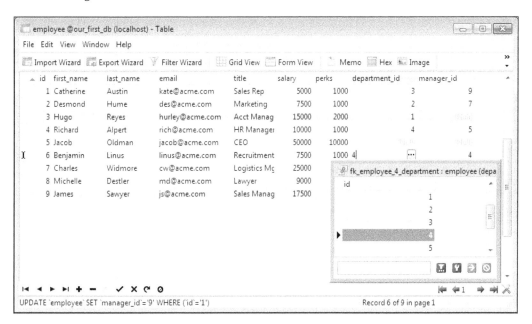

If you used Microsoft Access or Oracle Forms before, the form view will look familiar to you. Every table row or record will be displayed on a separate page with the fields aligned vertically in that view. Refer to the following screenshot:

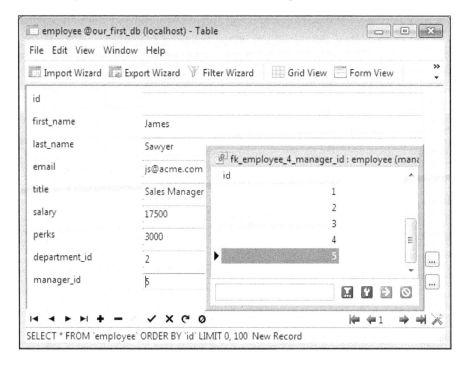

Creating views

Database views are usually used to hide complex details of certain tables and in some cases, they're used simply as a security mechanism by limiting the data that a user is allowed to retrieve. In this section, I'll show you how to create a view, in a moment, using Navicat's view designer. It has a powerful visual editing tool called the **View Builder** and it allows you to design views visually using point-and-click and drag-and-drop gestures.

To add a table to the view, simply click on its name on the left pane, and drag it to the graphical view area, or just double-click on its name in the tree view and click on **View Builder** tab and then follows these steps:

1. When you get all your tables in the graphical view, you can click on the tiny boxes next to the field names on the left-hand side to include them in the view. If you click on the box on the left-hand side of the table name, all the fields will be included in the **SELECT** query of the view, as shown in the following screenshot:

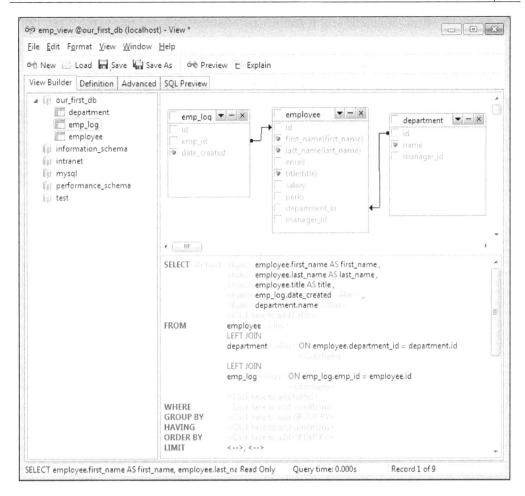

2. To define the relationships, click on the name of a field of a table and drag it onto the field of the table it is related to. For example, in this view, we want to display the name of the department of every employee instead of his/her department ID.

3. Click on the **department_id** field in the **employee** table and drag it onto the **id** field of the **department** table. A connecting line will be drawn representing the relationship between the two tables.

   In the meantime, the SQL representation of the visual design will be updated accordingly in the lower-right pane, which is called the syntax view. The relationships will be created as **INNER JOIN** by default; however, you can change them to **LEFT JOIN** or **RIGHT JOIN** by clicking on its SQL syntax highlighted in blue, and selecting a different join type from the menu that pops up.

Alternatively you can switch to the **Definition** tab of the view designer to work with plain SQL. You can switch between the two any time, as it is possible to generate the SQL query from the visual design and vice versa. However, make sure you save your view definition at every step and even back up the SQL to an external file at every major step as it is possible that the SQL query gets mixed up when trying complex things in the visual editor.

For our example, enter the following SQL query in the **Definition** pane:

```
SELECT
employee.first_name AS `first name`,
employee.last_name AS `last name`,
employee.title AS title,
emp_log.date_created AS `date joined`,
department.`name` AS `department`
FROM
employee
LEFT JOIN department ON employee.department_id = department.id
LEFT JOIN emp_log ON emp_log.emp_id = employee.id
```

To preview the results of the generated SQL, click on the **Preview** button on the toolbar. You will see the data retrieved by the view in a tab called **Result1**, if your SQL statement had no errors.

The **Explain** button on the toolbar shows the query plan of the view.

For power users, there's also a tab titled **Advanced**, where you can set advanced properties for the view. One of them is the **Algorithm**, and it gives you the ability to force MySQL to use a specific algorithm when executing the SQL.

- The default is **Undefined**, which leaves the choice to MySQL

- As the **Merge** algorithm is more efficient in most cases; it is the one MySQL picks whenever possible

- The alternative is the **Temptable** algorithm that retrieves the results after caching them in a temporary table

The **Security** option lets you customize access privileges by choosing between the user who defined the view and the one who invoked it.

More details about these settings are available in Navicat's manual.

When you double-click on a view you saved, you will get the results in a grid window, which is very similar to opening tables for viewing or entering data. From this window, it's possible to export the data in a variety of formats. The details of this functionality are covered in *Chapter 3, Data Management with Navicat.*

The created **View** will look like the following screenshot:

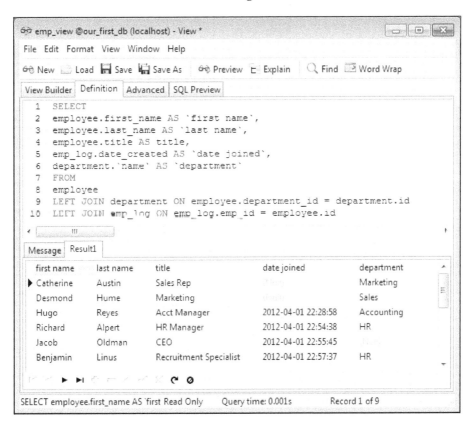

Working with functions and procedures

MySQL has brought support for functions and stored procedures as of Version 5. A stored procedure is a set of SQL statements that can be stored on the server, so that they can be invoked later by a client, a trigger, or even another stored procedure.

Now, we will create a simple stored procedure that will select the employees with the lowest, highest, and average salaries in the company.

The default way of creating such a routine in Navicat is through the **Function Wizard** that is invoked by clicking on the **New function** button in the toolbar or by selecting the **New Function** command from the pop-up menu showing up with a right-click on the appropriate context.

In the **Function Wizard** window, select **Procedure** and click on **Next**.

Then enter the following parameters for the procedure before you click on **Finish**:

Mode	Name	Type
OUT	lowest_salary	**decimal(10,2)**
OUT	l_emp	**varchar**
OUT	highest_salary	**decimal(10,2)**
OUT	h_emp	**varchar**
OUT	average_salary	**decimal(10,2)**

After entering the parameters in the previous table, the screenshot will look like the following:

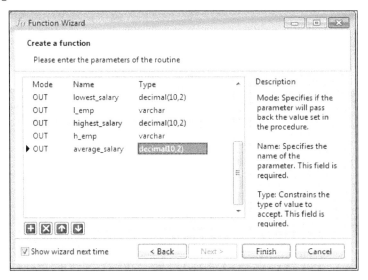

After clicking on **Finish**, the created **Procedure** will look like the following:

Finally, enter the following code in the routine's **Definition** on the next screen and save the procedure as `sp_salaries`.

```
BEGIN
SELECT Min(salary) INTO lowest_salary FROM employee;
 SELECT CONCAT_WS('' '', first_name, last_name) INTO l_emp FROM em
ployee WHERE salary = lowest_salary;
 SELECT Max(salary) INTO highest_salary FROM employee;
 SELECT CONCAT_WS('' '', first_name, last_name) INTO h_emp FROM em
ployee WHERE salary = highest_salary;
 SELECT Avg(salary) INTO average_salary FROM employee;
END
```

While entering the previous code, you can enjoy the code editing capabilities of Navicat, such as the code highlighting, word wrapping, auto-completion, and code-folding.

Now, in order to test the procedure, go to the **Queries** node, create a **New Query**, and then enter the following statements in the **Query Editor**:

```
CALL sp_salaries(@lowestsalary, @low_emp, @highestsalary, @high_emp,
@averagesalary );
```

```
SELECT @lowestsalary, @low_emp, @highestsalary, @high_emp, @
averagesalary;
```

To see the results of the query, click on the **Run** button in the toolbar and there we are with the lowest and highest paid employee in the company, their salaries, and the average salary of all employees in the company.

Lastly, since we don't have a single field for the full name of employees and instead have separate fields for first name, we will create a function that returns the full name of an employee by concatenating his/her first name and last name delimited with a single space character whose ID is taken as an input parameter.

To do this, we'll follow almost the same steps from the beginning of this section, except that in the first screen of the **Function Wizard**, we'll select **Function** instead of **Procedure**.

Next, we'll specify `emp_id` of type **int** as the input parameter and click on **Finish**. Finally, in the function's **Definition** area, enter the following code:

```
BEGIN
    DECLARE fullname VARCHAR(50);
    SELECT CONCAT(first_name, '' '', last_name) INTO fullname
    FROM employee WHERE id = emp_id;
    RETURN fullname;
END
```

Save the function as `fn_fullname` and test it by clicking on **Run** on the toolbar. When prompted, enter **id** of an employee whose full name you want to display. Refer to the following screenshot:

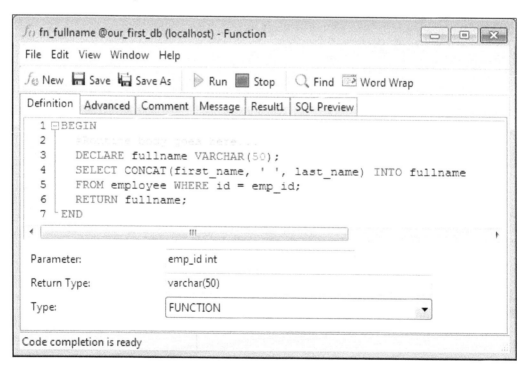

Using Navicat's event designer for MySQL

As of Version 5.1.6, the **Event Scheduler** feature of MySQL was introduced, which lets you design scheduled tasks. An event in MySQL is a scheduled task consisting of one or more SQL statements to be executed at certain intervals, beginning, and ending at specific dates and time.

In this section, I'll show you how to create a scheduled event that will back up our employee table, which will recur at specific intervals. As a prerequisite, we need to make sure that MySQL's global event scheduler is active (which is disabled by default).

For this, select **Console** from the **Tools** menu in Navicat's main window to get a command-line access to the MySQL server, as shown in the following screenshot:

While in the **localhost - Console** prompt, type the following command:

```
mysql> SET GLOBAL EVENT_SCHEDULER=ON;
```

Secondly, we will need to create a new stored procedure that will contain a set of commands to back up the employee table and delete any existing backup.

Time to put into practice what you have learned in the previous section:

1. Create a new stored procedure called `refresh_employee_bu` with no in or out parameters and enter the following code in its definition:

```
BEGIN
DROP TABLE IF EXISTS employee_backup;
    CREATE TABLE employee_backup LIKE employee;
    ALTER TABLE `employee_backup`
    MODIFY COLUMN `id` int(11) NOT NULL FIRST;
    INSERT employee_backup SELECT * FROM employee;
END
```

2. Now we're ready to create a scheduled event in Navicat; click on the **Event** button in the toolbar, then select **New Event**. This will bring in Navicat's event designer.

3. While in the **Definition** tab of the event designer, set the **Definer** as root@localhost or CURRENT_USER if you had established the connection using root. Set **Status** to **ENABLE**, and select **PRESERVE** for **ON COMPLETION**, as shown in the following screenshot:

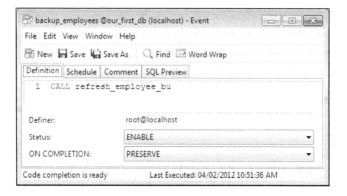

4. Then enter the following code in the definition code area: CALL refresh_employee_bu. This will invoke the stored procedure you created earlier for backing up the employee table.

5. Finally, switch to the **Schedule** tab of the event designer to adjust the timing of the event, as shown in the following screenshot:

We want the backup process to run every month, so refer to the previous screenshot to adjust your settings so that the event will be triggered every month, **STARTS** at **CURRENT_TIMESTAMP** + 1 hour **INTERVAL**. Save this event as `backup_employees` and you're done.

 To test if the scheduled event is working, you can set a much sooner date and time and shorter interval for a start, and then once you verify it's working, you can set the timing back to a reasonable frequency.

Working with queries in Navicat

Designing a query in Navicat is much like designing a view except that views are limited to SELECT statements whereas the queries can perform any CRUD (**create**, **read**, **update**, and **delete**) operation.

Just like the **View Builder**, Navicat's visual query builder allows you to graphically represent tables and fields as well as relationships between them (JOINS) and by leaving the SQL generation to Navicat, however, this approach only works with SELECT queries. You still have to handcode the SQL for create, update, and delete queries.

In this section, we'll go through an imaginary scenario regarding the fictional company `Acme.com`, where the CEO is unhappy with the financial results from the past fiscal year and believes that the company's organization should be revised. Toward this end, he wants preliminarily analysis of who's doing what and how much salary he or she gets in the company.

First, we will design a simple query to list all departments and their managers.

Designing the Query

Let's go to the **Queries** view by either clicking on the large **Query** button on the toolbar or by selecting **Queries** from the navigation pane on the left-hand side, and then click on the smaller **New Query** button on the toolbar.

In the window that opens, the **Query Editor** tab is active by default. This is where you can handcode the SQL language to construct a query. What we want is the visual designer, so we'll switch to the **Query Builder** tab.

In this view, we have a visual diagram pane where we can create graphical representations of tables and views by either double-clicking on their names on the left pane, or simply by moving them to the empty area using drag-and-drop gestures.

For this query, we need **department** and **employee** tables side-by-side; so after bringing them to the stage, start building a SELECT query by choosing the following fields by clicking on the tiny boxes next to their names: **name** of the **department** table, **first_name**, **last_name**, and **title** of the **employee** table.

Next, click on **manager_id** of the **department** table and move it onto the **id** field of the **employee** table. A line with round ends bonding the two fields should appear, and in the pane below an editable SQL code is previewed. You can click on the gray words in the SQL query to make additions to the syntax, such as aliases for fields and tables. This query is now almost ready except that I want a **LEFT JOIN** between **department** and **employee** instead of an **INNER JOIN** here. Click on the blue **INNER JOIN** expression to change it to a **LEFT JOIN** using a drop-down list that will show up automatically, as shown in the following screenshot:

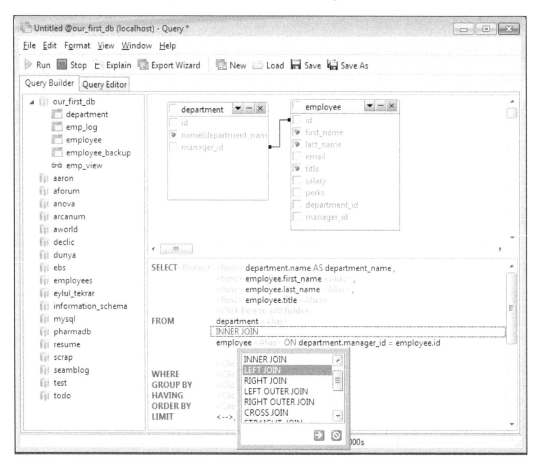

Now let's save this query and execute it to find out about the organization of the company. I named it `qry_departments`.

Click on the **Run** button on the window's toolbar to execute the query. Invoking it will switch back to the query editor and retrieve the results in a data grid below the generated SQL code. At this stage, we have the option of exporting the resulting data to a variety of formats, such as text (csv), Excel spreadsheet, XML, MS Access database (Windows only), or even a DBase file. Details of importing/exporting data functionality of Navicat are covered in *Chapter 3, Data Management with Navicat*. Refer to the following screenshot:

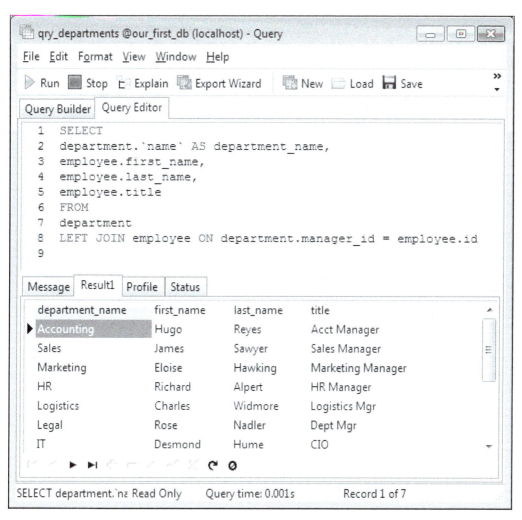

Unlike other database objects, Navicat does not prompt you to save your query when you are closing the query designer window, so be sure to save your work to avoid losing your changes.

Building further queries

Having designed our first query in the previous section, I think that we could spice up what we have learned by adding some more to it.

Going back to our scenario, the boss wants a list of employees (specifically the managers) with a monthly salary amount of more than $15,000, which department they work in, and who they report to. That's the specification of the next query we will design. If you are good at SQL programming, you could conceive such a query in a matter of minutes just by handcoding. Navicat's code editor is very useful also for this kind of task, thanks to its code-completion aid, SQL formatting, code folding, and brace highlighting. However, I want to demonstrate a few more features of the visual builder for the sake of the ease-of-use it provides for setting filtering criteria. For this query, we'll be working with the **department** table to retrieve the names of departments associated with the department ID of employees, and two instances of the **employee** table—one for the employees themselves and the second one to fetch the names of their managers.

Open a new query window and add two **employee** tables and one **department** table to the (graphical) diagram view area by dragging them from the left pane or double-clicking on their names. Name the second **employee** table as **manager** using an alias. You can do this either by double-clicking on the table's title bar or by clicking on the slightly dimmed **<Alias>** in the syntax view, and entering **manager**. (The former method is similar to renaming a file by clicking on its name under or next to its icon in Windows Explorer or the Macintosh Finder.) Refer to the following screenshot:

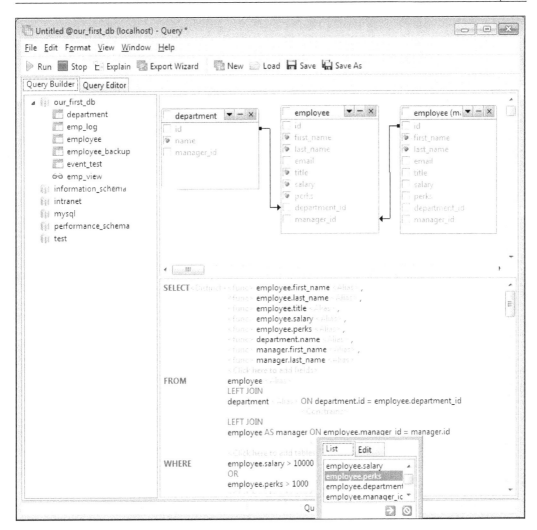

Connect the **department** table to the **employee** table by associating **id** of the
department table to **department_id** of the **employee** table, and then connect the
employee table to the **manager** table by associating **manager_id** of the **employee** table
to **id** of the **manager** table. Convert these associations to **LEFT JOIN** instances, so that
we also retrieve the employees who are not assigned to any manager or a department.

Next, select the following fields: **first_name** of the **employee** table, **last_name** of the **employee** table, **title** of the **employee** table, **salary** of the **employee** table, **perks** of the **employee** table, and **name** of the department table for the query.

Now we need to specify two conditions: **employee.salary** must be greater than 15,000 or **employee.perks** must be greater than 1,500.

To add a condition in the visual editor, click on the symbol group **<--> = <-->** from the **WHERE** clause in the syntax view. Click on **<-->** to choose the field from the list of all the table fields, available in the query. To define your own criteria, you can type your values directly in the **Edit** tab. Click on the equals sign (**=**) to change the condition operator.

Now if we execute the query, we'll get more or less of what we wanted; all the employees with salaries over $15,000 or perks over $1,500. But the CEO is also on the list. Besides, the result sheet is not very appealing to the eye with some of the bizarre column names and with the first names and last names appearing in different columns. While in the query editor, we shall manually edit the SQL to address these issues while enjoying the comfort of Navicat's code editor.

I think it's a good idea to concatenate the first and last names to show them in a single column, change the column title of department names to something sensible, exclude the CEO from the query results by adding another condition to the query, and sort the results by the amount of salaries in descending order.

To achieve these little goals, we'll modify the SQL to resemble the following code listing and re-run the query:

```
SELECT
CONCAT_WS('' '',employee.first_name,employee.last_name) AS FullName,
employee.Title,
CONCAT(''$ '',FORMAT(employee.salary,2) ) AS Salary,
employee.Perks,
department.`name` AS Dept,
CONCAT_WS('' '',manager.first_name,manager.last_name) AS ManagerName
FROM employee
LEFT JOIN department ON department.id = employee.department_id
LEFT JOIN employee AS manager ON employee.manager_id = manager.id
WHERE
```

```
(employee.salary > 15000 OR
employee.perks > 1500) AND
employee.title <> ''CEO''
ORDER BY employee.salary DESC, employee.perks DESC
```

Navicat also provides us with the ability to show the query profile and status, thanks to which we can monitor certain status parameters, such as table locks, system locks, and statistics under the **Profile** tab in the query results window. Refer to the following screenshot:

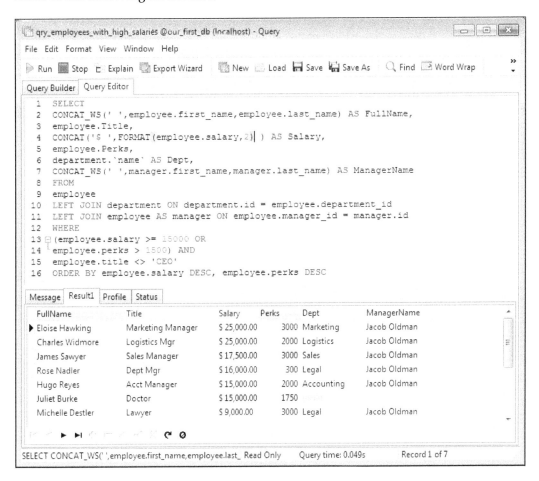

Summary

In this chapter, we have covered a great deal of database features from Navicat and we learned how to create and manage database objects using Navicat's visual tools.

We now know how to make use of Navicat's GUI tools to:

- Create a database and perform its initial setup
- Create and manage database objects such as tables and views
- Define foreign key constraints and triggers
- Create stored procedures and functions
- Schedule tasks using MySQL events
- Design and customize queries

In the next chapter, we will see in detail Navicat's data management tools and learn how to manipulate and transform databases easily using Navicat.

3
Data Management with Navicat

In the past, some of us would work with a database and its contents the hard way, typing commands in a console window or using primitive GUI tools with limited functionality. When it came to migrating a database from one server to another or even a simple restore from a backup, such stunts could become tedious tasks. In this chapter, we will see how easy and less time-consuming it is to perform all these tasks with Navicat.

Also, we will manipulate big chunks of data using Navicat's sophisticated tools, and you will learn how to:

- Import and export data using a variety of formats, such as XML, Excel files, `.csv`, and `.sql`
- Direct data transfer between different databases
- Synchronize data and structure
- Back up a database for restoring later
- Create and schedule batch jobs

Working with an existing database

From this point on, we'll work with an existing sample database called Sakila. Apart from being the name of the dolphin in the MySQL logo, Sakila is an example of a movie database developed by Mike Hillyer—a former member of the MySQL AB documentation team—and is intended to provide a standard schema that can be used, for example in books, tutorials, and articles. It also serves to highlight the features introduced in MySQL 5.x, including views, stored procedures, and triggers. The default installation of MySQL 5.5 Community Edition includes a copy of Sakila along with another sample database named World. If you already have a version of the MySQL server (earlier than 5.5) installed on your computer and do not want to upgrade for specific reasons, we have included a copy of the dump file of the Sakila database in the example code for this book. You can also download it from `http://dev.mysql.com/doc/index-other.html`. Once you arrive at the page, select the **Other Docs** tab and look in the **Example Databases** section. There you can find other sample databases too, with which you can experiment and apply what you will have learned through this chapter, as shown in the following screenshot:

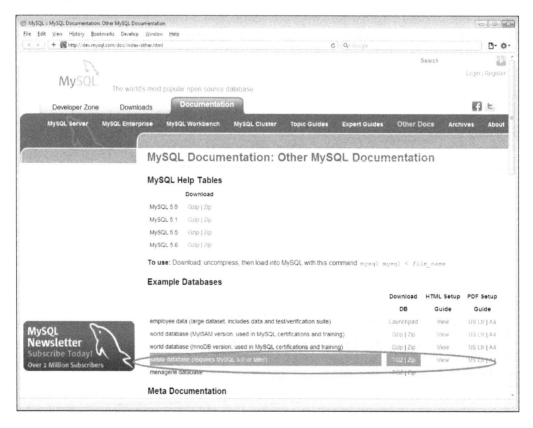

Once you have downloaded Sakila's compressed archive (either in `.zip` or `.tgz` format) and extracted its contents, you will find three files, which are called SQL dump files, in a folder called `sakila-db`. We need only two of them—`sakila-schema.sql` and `sakila-data.sql`. We'll use `sakila-schema.sql` in order to generate the Sakila database on our MySQL server; all the tables, views, functions, and stored procedures, which constitute the database structure, will be created. The other file, `sakila-data.sql`, will populate the data of the Sakila database.

Creating the database schema from a SQL dump file

Now, to generate the Sakila database on your server, I need you to right-click on **localhost** (or whatever server you defined a connection for) from the **Connections** pane of Navicat's main window and follow these steps:

1. Select **Execute SQL file...** from the contextual menu that pops up, as shown in the following screenshot:

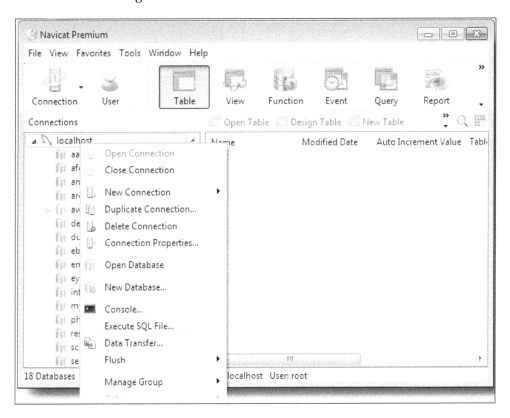

2. A new, smaller window will then open up with two tabs, where you will specify the SQL file to execute action queries from, in this case, SQL commands, to create the database and its objects. While under the **General** tab of the **Execute SQL File** window, click on the small, square-shaped button at the right end of the field labeled **File**, to choose `sakila-schema.sql`.

3. If the other settings in this window look like what you see in the screenshot, such as the **Encoding** which should be **65001 (UTF-8)**, you can directly proceed to click on the **Start** button.

Optionally, you could uncheck **Continue on error** to make sure your settings are correct before Sakila is generated on your machine as it's supposed to be; and if not, the operation will be broken and you will know in advance that you need to recheck the settings regarding your database server installation and connection properties. In other words, the operation should go just fine with the default settings, but in the event of any error during the execution of the queries — probably resulting from a possible misconfiguration — it's best to stop creating the database and revise the settings by referring to the previous chapter.

Alternatively, you can leave the **Continue on error** option checked and execute all the queries in the SQL file. In the case of any error, you can refer to the **Message Log**, which is under the second tab of this window. Refer to the following screenshot:

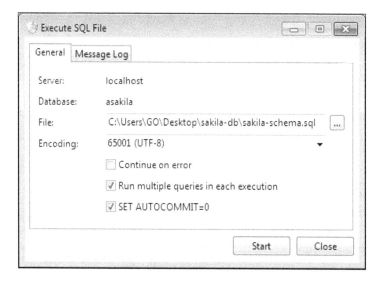

4. After you finish executing the SQL file, you will automatically be switched to the **Message Log** tab, as shown in the following screenshot:

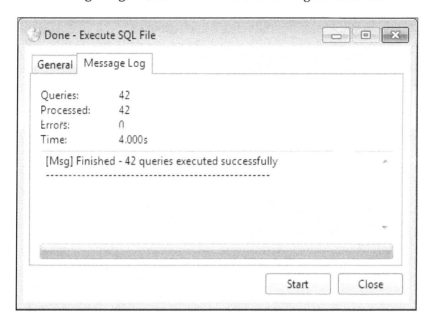

5. At this stage, there's the option of starting over by clicking on the **Start** button again, or by closing the window.

6. Going back to Navicat's main window, there appears to be no change. Now what? Nothing to worry about; we just need to refresh the view to see our newly created Sakila database and its objects. Right-click on **localhost** again, and select **Refresh** from the pop-up menu (On the Mac, it's labeled as **Refresh Connection**).

This is one of the most powerful features of Navicat. In just a few seconds, we executed a SQL dump file to recreate a database without having to type commands in a console window or having to go through complicated screens, as shown in the following screenshot:

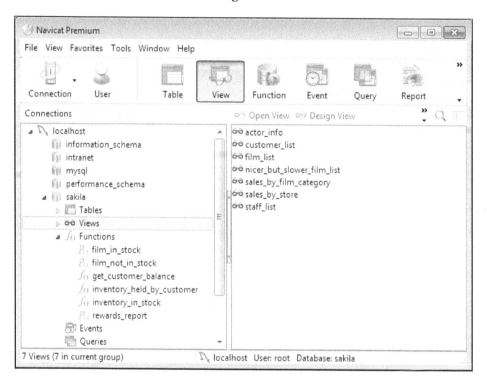

All the **Tables**, **Views**, **Functions**, and stored procedures are now listed in the main window. Click on **Tables** to see what we've got. We have almost every element that we would find in a typical relational movie database such as film, actor, category, staff, and some association tables, which are also called junction tables, such as **film_actor** and **film_category**. Double-click on some of them to see what they look like in Navicat. There are some custom views as well, such as **nicer_but_slower_film_list** and **sales_by_film_category**.

The first thing you will notice, however, is that these **Tables** and **Views** are all empty, without data. It's because the .sql file we executed contains only the database structure. So we have only created the blank database schema, and we need to repeat the steps in the beginning of this section to execute the other SQL dump file called sakila-data.sql, which contains the data to populate the database.

Now that we have the full database, with a complete structure, at our disposal, it's time to fill it with some data.

Right-click on the **sakila** database from the tree view in the left pane, make sure it's connected by verifying if its little cylinder-like icon is green, and then select **Execute SQL file** from the pop-up menu. This time, choose sakila-data.sql and click on **Start**. The title of the auxiliary window should become something like **Execute SQL file**, and the **Message Log** tab should read **[Msg] Finished - 56 queries executed successfully**.

Importing and exporting data

In the previous section, we have actually imported the **sakila** database by using SQL dump files. In this section, we'll cover import/export capabilities of Navicat in more detail.

As our first exercise, we will export **our_first_db**, the database that we created in *Chapter 2*, *Working with Databases*, in a .sql file, so that it can be regenerated on another MySQL server or as another instance of the database on the same server. To export **our_first_db**, follow these steps:

1. Right-click on **our_first_db** and choose **Dump SQL file...** from the pop-up menu. (If that menu item is dimmed and therefore inactive, you can first select **Open Database** from the same pop-up menu and then proceed with the intended step by right-clicking on it again.)

2. Finally, indicate the path where you want the SQL dump file to be created and by what name you want it to be saved in the **Save as** dialog box, and click on **Save**. Your database will be exported or dumped into a .sql file, which, when executed as described in the previous section, will be regenerated exactly with the same structure and data you created, as shown in the following screenshot:

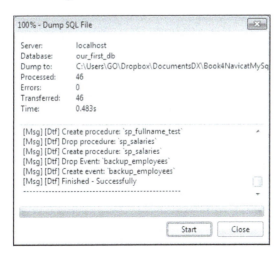

The previous procedure is one step away from exporting an entire database, although there are other variants of data exporting methods in Navicat, which will be covered in a moment, in this chapter. The **sakila** database, for example, came in two, separate, .sql files—one for the schema and the other for the data. If you export **sakila** using the same method, which is, by running the **Dump SQL file** command, Navicat will export the entire database in a single dump file.

One thing to know about Navicat's way of exporting SQL dump files is that Navicat does not include a command to create the database, such as CREATE DATABASE db_name, in the file.

Therefore, before executing dump files created by Navicat, you should first select a database or create a new one, and then proceed with the execution to generate the schema and to populate the data, if any.

If you are going to use the exported .sql dump file in a different administration tool, such as phpMyAdmin or MySQL Workbench, you should manually add the SQL command that would create the database. For example, you could add a line with the code CREATE DATABASE our_first_db in the beginning of the file, using a text editor.

Another one of Navicat's most acclaimed features is its ability to export data to a variety of formats. Some of the major ones will be covered in a moment.

Exporting in detail

If you are a database administrator or some sort of an IT analyst, you might often receive business requests to provide your client with an output of a table or a query from a database on the company intranet, typically in the Microsoft Excel format. In such cases, Navicat comes extremely handy for exporting the needed data and in a wide range of exporting options.

You can open any **Table**, **View**, or **Query**, and then click on the **Export Wizard** button on the toolbar of the window. When you do that, Navicat asks you if you want to export all the data in the table (in the Windows version).

Now this part is a bit tricky. First of all, *the table* in the expression **all the data in the table** refers to what kind of database object you're dealing with. When you're exporting the results of a **View** or **Query**, then **export all the data in the table** means all the data in the result list of the **View** or the **Query** you have been working on. Secondly, **all the data** means all the records in the database table, even if you displayed a limited amount of data. Please note that Navicat displays, at most, a thousand rows by default, when displaying the contents of a **Table**, **View**, or **Query**, in order to prevent a heavy workload on the database server.

This limit can be changed or removed by clicking on a tiny toolset icon at the bottom-right of the results window, which is shown in the following screenshot:

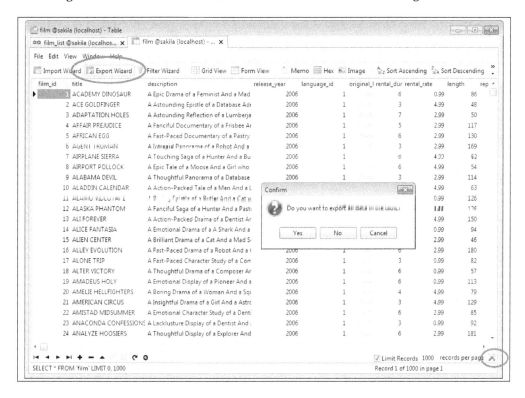

To see this in action, follow these steps:

1. Go to the **Tables** in the **sakila** database, and double-click on the table named **film**. You should see a list of movies with details such as the **title**, **description**, **release_year**, and so on.

2. Click on the toolset icon at the bottom-right to set the limit for the number of results shown in the previous screenshot. The database, **sakila**, contains a thousand titles in the films table anyway, so set the limit to 500 before you test how many rows will be exported in the next step.

3. Now, click on the **Export Wizard** button on the toolbar (alternatively an **Export Wizard** command is also available in the **File** menu), and then click on **Yes** when you are prompted with **Do you want to export all data in the table?**.

   You will be presented with the **Export Wizard** window, where you will need to specify the export file format with options ranging from the **Dbase** file format to **MS Access database** or **Excel spreadsheet** to **XML**.

While the Windows version of Navicat provides a plethora of file format options to choose from, the Mac version presents fewer options for the export file format (which explains why the Mac version is slightly cheaper). To be specific, CSV, plain text, XML, Dbase file (.dbf), and Excel formats are the file formats. You can refer to the following screenshot, which contains screenshots from both the Mac and the Windows versions of Navicat. This screenshot compares the differences of the user interface elements, such as the toolbar and the icons as well as file exporting options:

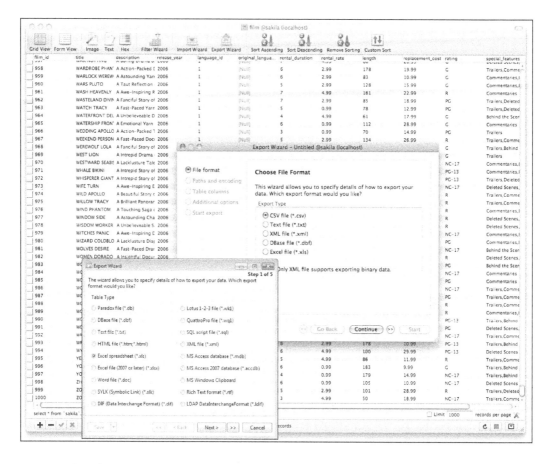

Another point to be aware of when exporting to Excel is that the version of the spreadsheet that will be created depends on which version of Microsoft Excel is installed on your computer.

4. After you select the desired output file format, you can click on **Next** in Windows (or simply the **Continue** button in the Mac version) for the next step, where you will be setting the destination filename, the encoding, and a few more options.

Even if you started the export operation on a single table output, this step lets you choose other tables in the database to export to separate files (unless you clicked **No** when prompted to export **all the data,** in the first place); that is, you can export each table to a separate file, as shown in the following screenshot:

What's more is you can even export more than one table (or all) to a single file. This is done simply by specifying the same filename (and path) for each source table in the corresponding field under the **Export to** column. This approach has different consequences depending on the file format you have chosen in the first place. For example, if you choose to export two or more tables to a single Excel file (.xlsx), each will be a separate spreadsheet in the same file.

To set the encoding of the file that will be exported, click on the **Advanced** button to display a little pop-up dialog window. The default **Encoding** is pertinently **65001 (UTF-8)**, which you can change from the drop-down list.

Under the **Encoding** selection box, there is also a checkbox to add a timestamp as a suffix to the exported filename. This is very useful to distinguish between the files in cases where you perform this task very often and end up accumulating a stack of exported files in a folder with identical names. You can even choose between different date patterns, such as **YYYY-MM-DD-HHNNSS** and **MM-DD-YYYY** for the time stamp, which will add a suffix to the output filename.

> In the Windows version of Navicat, you have two options for exporting to Excel. One of them is **Excel spreadsheet (*.xls)**, which is also the only available option in the Mac version. The second is **Excel file (2007 or later) (*.xlsx)**. With the former option, you cannot successfully export more than one source table into a single destination file, whereas the latter lets you achieve this as it uses some component on your computer installed with Microsoft Office. The Excel files you export using this option are created more slowly, but their version exactly matches the version of Office installed on your PC.

5. The next step is selecting the columns (or fields) for exporting by checking all the checkboxes of table, view, or query, by default. In order to omit some of them, simply uncheck **All Fields** first, and then uncheck the (un)desired fields listed under **Available Fields**.

   If you are exporting more than one table and want to specify a different selection of columns for each, you will need to repeat this step for each table you are exporting, by choosing from the drop-down list labeled **Source Table** and then checking/unchecking the field names in the list below it, which updates itself as you switch between tables.

6. In the next screen, you can specify whether or not you want an additional row at the top of the exported file containing the column titles. Also, you can opt to append exported records to an existing file. Also, you can check the option **Continue on error**, which will prevent the operation from halting in the event of an error.

You could be presented with additional options if you were exporting some other file format such as in the case of XML or text files, for example, where you specify settings, such as row and field delimiters, text qualifiers, and the format for date, time, and numbers.

 One of the best and foolproof ways to transfer or exchange data between MySQL and an Oracle or Microsoft SQL Database is by using the XML format when exporting data from a table.

7. When done, click on **Next** to go to the final step and start the export process. If you have chosen the .xls format instead of .xlsx, the exporting should be completed in a matter of seconds. When the operation is complete, you can perceive it from the progress bar and the **Message Log**.

Importing a file into a table

The same variety of file formats available for exporting a **Table**, **View**, or **Query** are also valid for importing data into a table. Excel spreadsheets, XML, and CSV files are among the most popular file formats used as data sources.

A business unit periodically sending an Excel spreadsheet to the IT department, with a request to update the corporate database with the information in its contents is one of the most common scenarios at work. And in some situations, the person who makes the spreadsheet often neglects to keep the column names consistent, for example, SALES_REP can become SALES_PERSON the next time and SALES_REP_NAME at another. Fortunately, Navicat prompts you to match the source columns with target fields, also giving you the flexibility to omit some or add additional ones.

When importing data from an Excel or CSV file, remember to correctly set field name row and first data row, which, typically, should not be the same.

In the example given in the screenshot, you can see the way additional actors are imported to the actor table from an Excel file, but some column names had to be manually matched for naming differences, such as **actor_id–actor_no** and **first_name–name**:

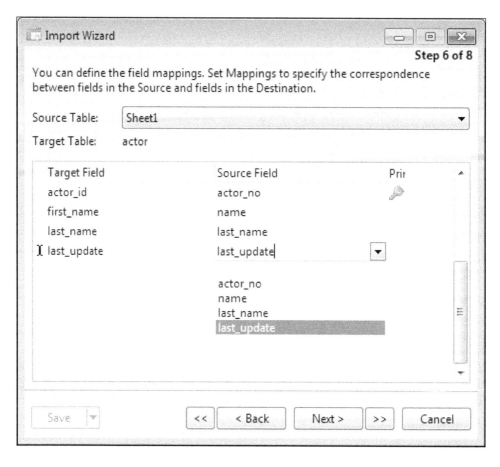

In addition to the popular data formats mentioned earlier, it is possible to import data from an ODBC data source in the Windows version of Navicat. This requires some knowledge of ODBC settings so as to be able to specify connection parameters. You can find detailed information for the ODBC import in Navicat's official manual.

Direct data transfer between two databases

Another flagship feature of Navicat is its capability to transfer database objects (**Tables**, **Views**, **Functions**, and **Events**) from one database to another, or to a SQL dump file. The target database can be on the same server or on another server. All you need to do is to have defined a connection to it as described in *Chapter 1*, *Getting Started*. The data transfer settings can also be saved as a profile for later retrieval or can be scheduled as a job.

You can start a data transfer process either by choosing **Data Transfer...** from **Tools** in the main menu bar, or by right-clicking on a database in the left navigation pane and selecting **Data Transfer...**. Once you initiate it, you can start specifying the settings in the **Data Transfer** window, as shown in the following screenshot:

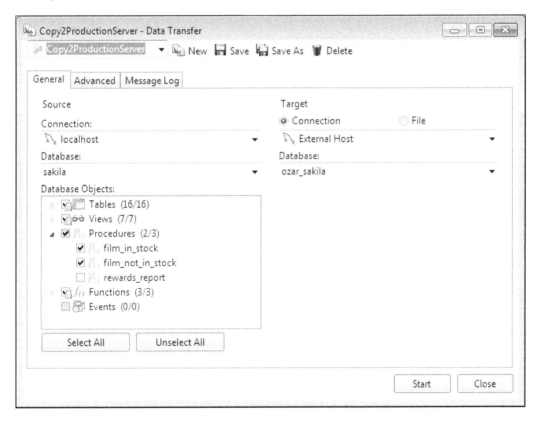

Although the interface here is fairly intuitive, with two main areas under the **General** tab categorized as **Source** and **Target** simply letting you choose which objects to transfer where, there are a few points to know before you get started, unless you want to learn how to use it by the hard way of trial and error. First, you need to have the target database ready beforehand, which means you need to at least have created a blank database as the target to receive the database objects, as Navicat (at the time of writing this) does not create the database itself but rather copies the objects to the specified target. You can also choose to transfer to an existing database already containing some objects, but in this case, you might want to make sure that they don't have the same names as those in the source unless you wish them to be overwritten or skipped.

Secondly, you can prefer to export to a SQL dump file, which is, in a way, similar to what I showed in the beginning of the chapter, except that on this screen, you are able to specify the SQL format ranging from MySQL 3.23 to 6.0 through file encoding.

If the target server version is different from that of your source, the direct transfer might fail, and you might have to resort to exporting a SQL file in this way.

The **Advanced** tab is where you can specify some additional settings, such as continuing on error and dropping target objects before creating. This means that any existing ones with the same name from the source will have been overwritten.

As with all the other utility windows of Navicat, click on **Start** to begin the process when you're done configuring the settings. The process can last from seconds to minutes, or even hours, depending on the size of the database, the amount of data, the distance between two servers, and your connection speed. I personally do not usually have to wait for a long time to transfer my blog's database from the server of my web hosting company, which is on another continent, and my blog has some 2,860 posts including comments.

Data and structure synchronization

If you have multiple instances of your database across different servers, for example, one for development, one for testing, and one other for production, it can be challenging that, for consistency, sometimes making a change in one (most likely in development) requires applying the exact same changes to the others. We as humans often make the mistake of neglecting one or more changes on all of the servers and end up with unexpected errors after deployment.

Navicat comes to the rescue in this area as well, with its structure and data synchronization wizards accessible from the **Tools** menu.

Another situation where the synchronization tools could be useful is in cases where a previously performed data transfer operation is not successfully completed. The target database can be retouched using structure and data synchronization afterwards.

The usage of both tools is more or less identical to the **Data Transfer** interface, where you can thoroughly designate which source and target database objects you want to be compared and in what detail. For example, in **Structure Synchronization**, you can opt to compare tables along with primary keys, foreign keys, and indexes, but also choose to exclude triggers, character set, and the auto-increment value under the **General** (**General Settings** on the Mac) tab. As such, you can specify your choice of the type of SQL commands to be executed by clicking on the appropriate checkboxes, as you have CREATE, ALTER, and DROP to choose from. You can even check an option to compare again after execution of the process. In the Windows version of Navicat, there is a button labeled **Compare** at the lower-right corner of the window. On the Mac version, the button is on the upper left-hand side in the window's toolbar with a scales icon. Click on it to begin the comparison of the structure of the source and target databases. Refer to the following screenshot:

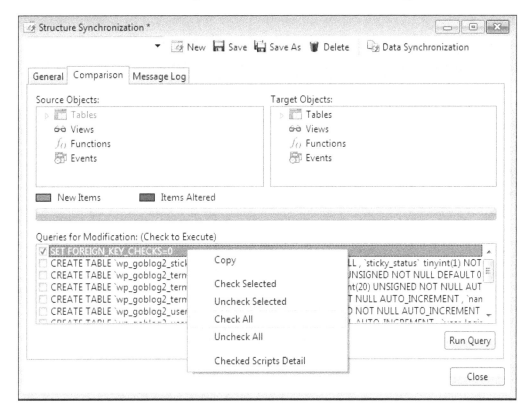

Next, we will need to go to the second tab named **Comparison** (**Compare Result** on the Mac), which will give us a sort of preview of what differences exist between the source and the target, and the SQL queries for synchronization will be listed as per the required modification in the second half of the window. You can individually select which queries are to be executed by clicking on their corresponding checkboxes, or click anywhere in the list to display a pop-up menu, which will allow you to select/unselect all, as well as copy the SQL syntax.

When you're done with it, click on **Run Query** to proceed. Then, you can watch the **Message Log** to see the results.

The **Data Synchronization** is slightly simpler where you simply select the source and target databases. Navicat automatically lists and matches the tables from both sides, so that you can verify if there's a correspondence for each table on both sides. Under the **Advanced** tab, you can specify whether or not you want to:

- Use transactions
- Show synchronization detail
- Insert records
- Delete records
- Update records

Lastly, you can click on **Preview** to see how data is going to get synchronized and then click on the **Start** button to let it actually happen, and see the executed commands in the **Message Log**.

Backup and restore

In case of a disaster, be it an electricity outage leading to a disk failure causing corruption of the database, or simply a user error of deletion of the wrong objects or data rows ending in data loss, it is crucial to back up your database. Navicat lets you back up all **Tables** (and their records), **Views**, **Functions**, and **Events** of your database for restoring later.

There's a big **Backup** button with a tape cassette icon on the toolbar of Navicat's main window, which will take you to a special view for managing backups, where a smaller toolbar appears under the main toolbar. This smaller toolbar has smaller buttons for creating a new backup, restoring a backup, or deleting it, plus a button for extracting SQL from the backups.

To create a new backup, follow these steps:

1. Click on the **New Backup** button from the object pane toolbar (in the Windows version), or right-click anywhere in the object pane itself and select **New Backup** from the pop-up menu (Windows & Mac).

2. In the window that appears, enter the properties of the backup you want to make, such as your own comment for the backup and the objects to be included in the backup. (All of the objects are selected by default.)

3. Then, click on **Start** to perform the backup with the specified settings.

Navicat also provides some advanced options here, such as compression, table locking, and the ability to use a single transaction for InnoDB tables.

 If you choose to use compression in the **Advanced** tab, a backup file with a .psc extension or with a .psb extension will be created.

Right-clicking on a backup and selecting **Object Information** from the pop-up menu will open an additional pane at the bottom of the window where you can see the size and full path of the file, as well as the last modification date. The backups are saved as single files in a hierarchy of subfolders under **My Documents**, by default. For example, my backups were stored in C:\Users\GO\Documents\Navicat\MySQL\ servers\localhost\sakila\sakila_bu.psc. You can copy or move a backup file in the .psc or .psb format to another computer just like working with any other file on Windows Explorer or Macintosh Finder.

Restoring a backup is even simpler. You can right-click on a backup from the list of your backups, and click on **Restore Backup** from the pop-up menu. To restore a backup that is created on another machine and copied to the computer you're using, click on the **Restore Backup** button on the toolbar. Otherwise, right-click on an empty area of the object pane and select **Restore Backup** from the pop-up menu, and select the backup file using the open file dialog box. Make sure you have the necessary privileges for the create, drop, and insert operations unless you're connected to the database with the **root** user.

For deleting an unwanted backup, you can also right-click on it and select **Delete**.

Backups can also be created from the command-line interface running the following commands:

Navicat Object	Command and parameter	File Extension
Backup	`Navicat.exe /backup ConnectionName DatabaseName`	
Backup Server	`Navicat.exe /backupserver ConnectionName`	`.psc` (compressed)/`.psb` (uncompressed)
Backup Database	`Navicat.exe /backupdatabase ConnectionName DatabaseName`	

Creating and scheduling batch jobs

The execution of a series of tasks on a computer or server without manual intervention is known as **batch processing**, and it is something that most DBAs do daily if not all the time. These tasks are called **jobs**, which are set up so that they run in the background unattended, with all the input data preselected through scripts or command-line parameters.

Navicat provides a similar functionality allowing you to create batch jobs and set schedules, which can be executed at defined intervals or at a specific date and time, or both.

Batch jobs can be created for query, report printing, backup, data transfer, data synchronization, and data import and export. You can define a list of actions to be executed within a single batch job, which can be run manually at will, or scheduled to run at a specified time or even periodically.

You can switch to the view related with batch jobs and schedules by choosing **View | Schedule** from the menu bar or pressing the button with the calendar icon in the main toolbar.

To create a new batch job, follow these steps:

1. Click on the empty area in the object pane.

2. Right-click and select **New Batch Job** from the pop-up menu, or click on the **New Batch Job** button from the object pane toolbar.

3. Enter the properties for the job that basically consists of selecting the actions to be performed, by selecting them from available jobs, putting them in the desired order, and specifying some advanced settings such as configuring e-mail notification, as shown in the following screenshot:

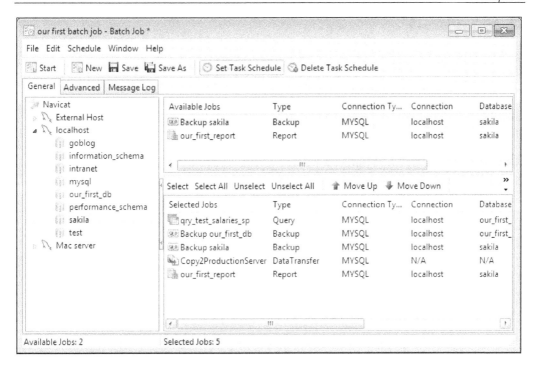

You can set the timing of the execution of this job by pressing the **Set Task Schedule** button on the toolbar. This brings in another pop-up window, where you can set the periods or frequency of the job under the **Schedule** tab, or specify the start date and the optional end date as well as the number of repetitions.

The **Advanced** tab lets you configure e-mail so that a user or a group of users can be notified of the results after the batch job is automatically run. It is even possible to attach a file output from Export Wizard or Data Transfer with the e-mail automatically generated and sent.

To create a batch job based on an existing one, select a job and then click on **Design Batch Job**, either on the object pane toolbar, or select it from the pop-up menu triggered by right-clicking on the job. After you finish your modifications, you can click on the **Save As** button on the toolbar of the editor window or Select **File | Save as...** from the menu bar.

Another quick and easy way of achieving the same result is by simply copying and pasting the job after selecting it and then performing the desired modifications on the duplicated job.

Summary

In this chapter, we have dealt with different techniques of data manipulation, transferring data from one database to another, and converting it to and from various file formats.

You have also learned to synchronize two instances of a database by means of both structure and data.

Backup and restore operations, as well as batch job creation and scheduling, are also essential in the lifecycle of a database (and in the life of a DBA) and you have learned how to use the fast and easy tools Navicat provides to accomplish these kinds of tasks.

In the next chapter, you will step into data modeling with Navicat.

4
Data Modeling with Navicat

As of version 10 of Navicat, a data modeler feature has been added to the application, which allows the user to create and edit database objects, such as tables, fields, and relationships in a visual editor.

PremiumSoft (the makers of Navicat) also released this feature as a separate application software product with the name **Navicat Data Modeler**, and it is available for Windows, Mac OS X, and Linux. For those who exclusively require a visual tool for data modeling and do not require the other administration and data management tools, which were covered in the previous chapters, Navicat Data Modeler could be a pertinent choice.

While Oracle's MySQL Workbench (a GUI administration and database modeling tool for MySQL) could be considered a free alternative, Navicat Data Modeler provides means for easier manipulation of model objects and also presents some advanced features, such as history tracking and database synchronization; thanks to this, you can asynchronously work with data diagrams for later synchronization with actual database structure(s). For a better understanding of the functionalities of Navicat modeling tools, we will begin the chapter by following a tutorial to design our first data model, in order to aid you in learning each feature step by step.

In this chapter, we will learn how to master Navicat's visual data modeling tool, which makes it easy to:

- Design data models in a GUI
- Create, edit, and manipulate table structures from within the visual editor
- Forward-engineer a data model into a `.sql` file
- Reverse-engineer an existing database into visual representations

Working with Navicat's model designer

Before we begin designing our first data model, it is a good idea to get acquainted with the tools that Navicat Data Modeler provides, which we have at our disposal.

The last button on the main toolbar in Navicat's main window is the **Model** button. Clicking on this button will take you to the model view. An alternative way is to select **Model** from the **View** menu (on the Mac, you can press the + key and the *8* key simultaneously as a shortcut). Then you can create a new blank model by right-clicking anywhere in the object pane of the main window and selecting **New model**.

On the Mac, press the + key and the *N* key simultaneously as a shortcut or click on the + button at the bottom-left side frame in the main window. On a Windows PC, simply click on the **New Model** button on the secondary toolbar, located under the main toolbar in the main window.

The screenshot of Navicat's toolbar on Mac and Windows is as follows:

This action also brings up a new window called **model designer**, where you can edit the data model. The left side pane of the **model designer** window contains the diagram of a tree palette that aids you to toggle its counterpart; a model tree palette is obtained by clicking on the tiny icons just above it. The diagram tree palette lists the model objects, such as tables, relationships, notes, and images (pictures) of the active diagram in alphabetical order. The model tree palette lists only the table objects of all the diagrams in the model. Now these metaphors can be extremely confusing, so I will describe briefly what each metaphor means and also explain their hierarchy.

Each model can contain one or more diagram that could also be called **entity-relationship diagrams** (**ER diagrams**) among database administrators. A database design can be split across the multiple diagrams within a model. There is also the concept of **layers**, but unlike graphics and image processing applications, layers in Navicat's Data Modeler are not containers or placeholders. Just like other objects, they are drawn on the canvas, but with a slight difference so that they are opaque and can be overlaid on other objects. Layers can be useful to organize certain objects by grouping the related ones and separating them according to different concerns. For example, when designing an ERP database, you may want to gather tables related with accounting and finance in one layer, and those related with sales and marketing in another.

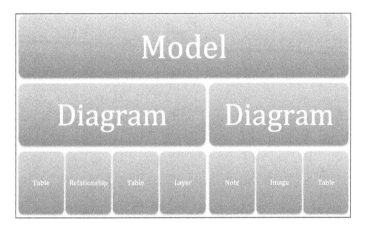

Aligned to the right-hand side of it is a vertical toolbar also called the model diagram palette, from which you can select the type of database object you want to place in the diagram. The available objects in this context are tables, notes (labels), pictures (images), layers, and relationships. The right side of the window contains the **Properties** palette (on the lower left-hand side in Windows), and it is used to display and edit the properties of the active diagram and the objects it contains. Here you can manage every setting, pertaining to the selected item in the canvas, with options to rename the diagram, adjust the number of pages (significant when printing), adjust the font and color of the labels of the objects, and the notation of the diagram. There are five notations available — **Default**, **Simple**, **IDEF1X**, **UML**, and **Crow's Foot**, respectively.

Below the **Properties** palette is **History Palette** (in the Mac version) that lists every action you performed step by step, allowing you to take these actions back by as many steps as you wish. There's also a preview pane on the opposite side, almost placed symmetrically, that you can use for a map-like navigation. In the Windows version, these two palettes are placed at each other's exact opposite location. Refer to the following screenshot of Navicat in the Mac version:

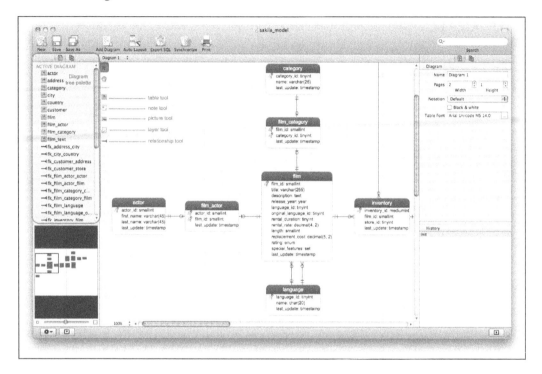

Creating our first model

This section features a tutorial in which we will create the model of a fairly **Simple To Do** application for the database. Our new database will consist of three tables—**tasks**, **categories**, and **users**. Using the model designer, we will design these tables and also define the field types, primary keys, and relationships. All of these three tables will be interrelated to each other using foreign keys. We will then annotate the model and finally generate the actual database, forward-engineering the model we will have created. To start working on the model, switch to the **model view** window(if you haven't already done so) by clicking on the large **Model** icon on the main toolbar of Navicat's main window; or select **Model** from the **View** menu, and then to create a new model, right-click on the empty area in the object pane and select **New Model** from the pop-up menu. In the Windows version of Navicat, you can also simply click on the **New Model** button from the smaller secondary toolbar,right under the main toolbar of Navicat's main window. In the Mac version, there is no secondary toolbar. Instead, on the lower frame, which is thick enough to fit a small button, there is a **+** sign. This **+** sign intuitively indicates the function of adding an object in the chosen context. In this case, a model is accompanied by two more buttons; one is with a **-** sign that means delete, the other with a pencil icon that means edit. (The Windows version has equivalent buttons explicitly labeled as **Design Model** and **Delete Model** respectively.) After you perform this step, a new model designer window named **Untitled–Model** will pop up, presenting you with a blank diagram named **Diagram 1**. Now, let's get ready to start editing the model by creating our first table in the diagram. Click on the **Table** button (a tiny button with a table-shaped icon) from the vertical model diagram toolbar, and then click on an empty area of the canvas. You could also right-click on the canvas and select **New | Table** from the pop-up menu. A new, square-like box with rounded corners will be drawn in the canvas right where you last clicked, with a blue title bar labeled as **Table 1** also highlighted, indicating that it's ready to be renamed for your convenience. In order to rename it, type `category` and press the *Enter* key. Next, right-click inside the box and select **Add Field** from the pop-up menu. (An alternative shortcut is to press the down arrow or the *Tab* key from your keyboard when editing a table or a field name.) You will notice a text cursor blinking inside the box representing the table.

Type `id` and press *Enter*. While Navicat is creating the field, it also senses what this field is meant for by the name you entered, and it automatically defines the field as a primary key of the **INTEGER** type. Now go on and repeat the previous step, this time typing `name` as the field name, and press *Enter*. Eureka! Navicat perceived this one correctly as well, and it created the field as a varchar type of 255 characters in length. The 255-character length is perhaps outrageous, but we'll see how to cut it down to size in a little bit. The ID and name fields are sufficient for the category table, so we are now moving onto the second table. Refer to the following screenshot to see how the tables, **category** and **task**, are created:

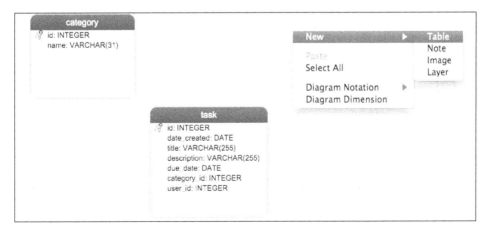

1. Create another table and name it `task`.
2. Add a field named `id` for this one as well (see how Navicat makes it another primary key of the **INTEGER** type).
3. Add the second field as `title` and press *Enter*. (Navicat will create this one of type **VARCHAR(255)**.)
4. In the same way, add the following fields—`description`, `due_date`, `category_id`, and `user_id`. (Navicat will determine what type they should be created of.)
5. Create one last table and name it `user`.
6. Create the following fields for it—`id`, `login_name`, `password`, `email`, and `role`.

Now, we need to fine-tune some of these fields. For example, we will trim the length of those varchar fields from a 255-character length to some more reasonable length. To do this, right-click on **task** and select **Design Table** from the pop-up menu. This will make a table designer interface very identical to the tables you saw in *Chapter 2, Working with Databases*. In Mac, the table will look similar to the following screenshot:

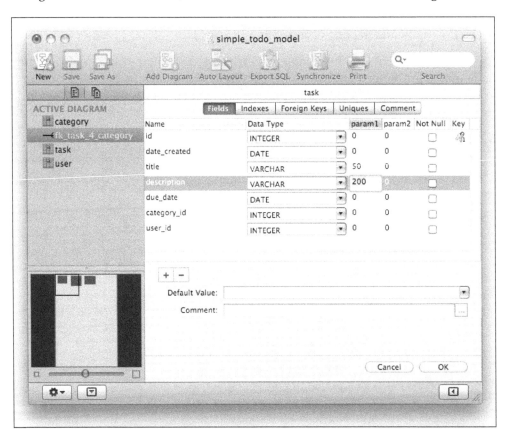

On this screen, you can add or remove fields, or rename them, change their data types, change the data length, assign or remove primary keys, define default values for fields, add indexes, and even add constraints such as foreign keys or uniqueness definitions.

You can even reorder the fields by gesturing the mouse to drag-and-drop the fields in this interface.

For this example, we will just reduce the length of the title to 50 and the description to 200.

You can refer to *Chapter 2, Working with Databases*, for more details on the table designer interface and the functionalities it provides, for editing and tweaking table structures.

Defining the relationships

Now that we have our three related tables, it is time to define the relationships between them. This model is intended for a **Simple To Do** database, where our main data would be stored in the **task** table. Every task to be entered here will have a title, description, entry date, due date, category, and user. Here we are storing the categories and users on separate tables, so we need to refer to the related category and user from the **task** table, using the ID columns. There is a many-to-one relationship between the **category** table and the **task** table. In our case, a task can have one category associated with it, but a category can have many tasks under it. As such, a task can be assigned to one user, but a user can have many tasks.

To establish a join between two tables, first select the relationship tool from the vertical palette, then move your pointer to the **task** table and click-and-drag the **category_id** field, dragging it onto the **id** field of the **category** table. This should establish the join between the two tables, and a line joining them on the canvas should appear.

But that's not all. What we have done so far is to establish a basic one-to-one relationship with no further information on the cardinality between the two objects, as shown in the following screenshot:

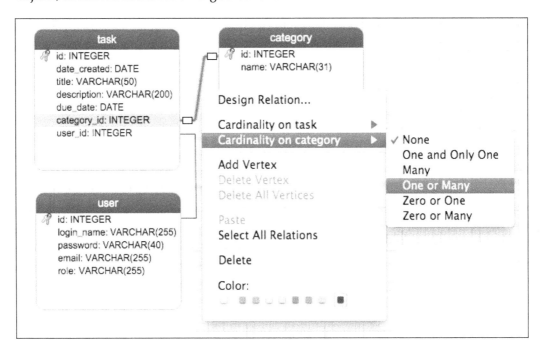

Now, to right-click on the adjoining line and then select **Cardinality on category | One or Many** from the pop-up menu. Now that a one-to-many relationship between the two tables is established, a foreign-key from **category** to **task** is automatically created; also, the category end of the joining line will have a fork-like joint in the diagram. One shortcoming of the diagram editor (directly editing on the canvas) is that when relationships are visually defined by point-and-click and drag-and-drop gestures, the joints of the lines may not be placed at the beginning or the end of referencing and the referenced fields. So, you will need to manually adjust them by clicking and dragging the joints to the correct location on the diagram object (of course, if you want more precision in the visual representation of these relationships).

We could have also used the **Design Relation...** command from the pop-up menu that is the equivalent of double-clicking on the joining line, which would bring us back to the table designer that has the **Foreign Keys** tab active. This is where you can fine-tune the foreign key definition of the adjoining table-field pairs; furthermore, it gives you the flexibility to reference more than one field in the join.

As you have seen, it is best to use on-canvas editing and the table designer in conjunction with one another, rather than as alternatives, to make the best of two worlds, and for maximum flexibility in data modeling. Refer to the following screenshot to see how **Foreign Keys** are created:

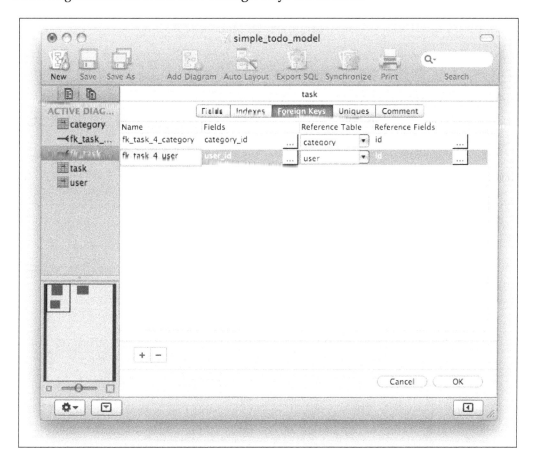

As many DBAs and software project managers would suggest (if not required), it is a good idea to conform to certain naming conventions when creating database objects, especially constraints such as **Foreign Keys**. I prefer to name **Foreign Keys** as starting with the prefix fk_ concatenated by the table name, and then with _4_ proceeded by the referenced table name, followed by the name of its primary key field. For example, in the case of the task-category relation, I used fk_task_4_category_id as the foreign key name, which means that this constraint is a foreign key defined for the **task** table that references the **id** field of the **category** table from the **category_id** field of the **task** table itself.

While Navicat provides a lot of ergonomie for database object management, especially for constraint and index management, many other tools do not. In case of a need for modification, it can become cumbersome for someone who is not using a sophisticated GUI tool to manage a database, to locate a foreign key or some other constraint in the database unless a certain naming standard is respected from beginning to end, and by everyone involved.

When you're finished editing, click on the **OK** button on the lower right-hand side of the screen to save your changes, or click on **Cancel** to discard them.

Adding some pizzazz to the model with notes and images

Imagine a case where you are designing a database model as part of a project proposal and you want your model to look pretty and appealing. Well, it could take more than a well-designed ER diagram to make your model seductive. The additional objects on the vertical model diagram palette, what I call annotation tools, can help you achieve just that.

Click on the tiny button with a yellow icon resembling a post-it note, on the vertical model diagram palette, to activate the note tool, and then click on an empty area of the canvas to drop in a sticky note. You can double-click on it to edit its text, as shown in the following screenshot:

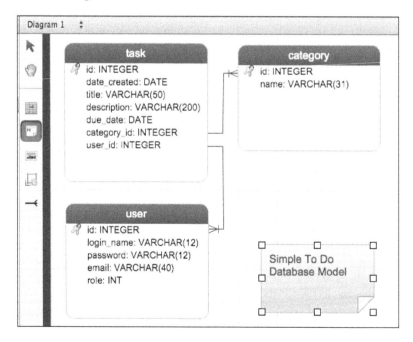

The note we have just added looks indeed like a post-it sticky, and it looks pretty good to me, in my humble opinion. But if you wish to change the appearance of the note (such as the color and text style), you can go to the properties pane and experiment with the different settings. The properties editor lets you tweak the note color, (rectangle) size, location, and even the font size and style.

If you prefer not to have a piece of sticky note on your model, but rather something more contemporary, you can choose to make the paper-like graphic completely disappear and leave only the text. To do this, simply click on the note with the arrow tool so it remains highlighted (or selected), and then in the properties pane select **Label** from the drop-down list named **Note style**. In Windows, right-click on the note and then go to **Style | Note**.

Right below the notes icon, there is the image tool with a tiny picture icon. You can add any picture or image to the diagram by first activating this tool by clicking on it, and by secondly clicking anywhere on the canvas. This will prompt you with your operating system's standard **Open** file dialog box, to select an image file or photo from your disk. Upon doing so, the image you have selected will be placed where you had clicked on the canvas. You could, for example, place your company logo in a corner to make the look and feel a little more corporate.

Working with layers

As mentioned earlier, the layers in Navicat's Model Designer are only for colorizing certain areas of the canvas for some kind of annotation, and can be used for marking a certain area of the canvas to gather some tables of a certain type of business logic. For example, you would want to separate the tables related with HR and put them within the boundaries of a certain layer, and put the tables related with manufacturing and logistics in another layer, for example, in a different area distinguished by a different layer, preferably in a different color, in the same diagram.

To create a layer, simply click on the icon above the relationship tool (and below the image tool) on the vertical palette, then click-and-drag a rectangular area of your choice on the canvas that you want your layer to be placed across.

 Please remember that layers are neither containers nor placeholders, and they serve no other purpose than being a visual aid.

Deleting unwanted objects

When you create a table in the model designer, it begins to exist both in the diagram and the model. Deleting a table from the diagram thereafter does not necessarily mean it will be deleted from the model, but the good news is that you are asked from what context you want to delete a table, provided that you right-click on the table and select **Delete | from Diagram** or **Delete | from Diagram and Model**.

What's the difference? Well, the decision affects the objects that will be created when you generate a database from a model design. At the end of this section, you will learn how to forward-engineer a database by generating SQL from the model design.

Objects other than tables and relationships have no impact on the database structure, so deleting them from a diagram also removes them from the model.

Working with multiple diagrams

As discussed in the beginning of the chapter, a model can contain multiple diagrams. Working with more than one diagram within a model can become necessary if you're working with very large databases, whose model would be too large to be managed, leaving you no choice but to divide them into subgroups and place them in separate diagrams.

We will not go into detail about working with more than one diagram within the same model. However, I want to mention a few points here. Also, the user interface of Navicat for Windows differs in some aspects from that of the Mac version, so I'll try to briefly explain the differences between the two user interfaces.

On both the Windows and Mac platforms, you can create a new diagram simply by clicking on the **New Diagram** button on the toolbar of the Model Designer window. When you do this on Windows, the new diagram comes up under a new tab right above the canvas area. You can switch between the diagrams simply by clicking on their tabs.

In the Mac version, instead of a tab bar on the top left side of the canvas, there's a drop-down menu labeled with the name of the active diagram. Also in the Mac version, at the bottom left side of every window, there is a small, black icon in the shape of toothed gear wheels. When clicked, it pops up a menu for you to add objects to, relevant to the context you're currently in. To switch between diagrams on the Mac, just click on its name and then select the name of the diagram from the drop-down menu that opens, which you want to toggle.

Exporting the model diagram to SQL

We have completed the design of a simple, yet functional, database model design. Now, it's time to put it to some use.

I mentioned earlier, the possibility of generating a database from a model. To achieve this with a model we designed from scratch, we first need to export our design to a .sql file.

On the Mac, there's a button labeled **Export SQL** on the toolbar of the Model Designer window. When you press it, the canvas is masked with an export settings form, where you must indicate which tables to export and optionally specify some advanced settings, such as excluding DROP statements, primary keys, indexes, and foreign keys from the generated SQL. You can leave these untouched if you don't want to omit anything.

In the Windows version, however, there's no export button on the toolbar; rather, you must select **Tools | Export SQL...** from the menu bar.

I suggest you uncheck the option of DROP statements, which could cause SQL errors, as this is the first time we'll be creating the **Simple To Do** database.

You can name the file to be exported something like simple-todo.sql and proceed with the exporting process.

Importing and exporting data was discussed in detail in *Chapter 3, Data Management with Navicat*.

The source code of the exported file should resemble the following:

```
CREATE TABLE category (
id INTEGER NULL,
name VARCHAR(31) NULL,
PRIMARY KEY (id)
);
CREATE TABLE task (
id INTEGER NULL,
date_created DATE NULL,
title VARCHAR(50) NULL,
description VARCHAR(200) NULL,
due_date DATE NULL,
category_id INTEGER NULL,
user_id INTEGER NULL,
```

```
PRIMARY KEY (id)
);
CREATE TABLE user (
id INTEGER NULL,
login_name VARCHAR(12) NULL,
password VARCHAR(12) NULL,
email VARCHAR(40) NULL,
role INT NULL,
PRIMARY KEY (id)
);
ALTER TABLE task ADD CONSTRAINT fk_task_4_category FOREIGN KEY
(category_id) REFERENCES category (id);
ALTER TABLE task ADD CONSTRAINT fk_task_4_user FOREIGN KEY (user_id)
REFERENCES user (id);
```

Finally, by applying what you have learned in *Chapter 2, Working with Databases* and *Chapter 3, Data Management with Navicat*, you can create a new database called **simple_todo** or just **todo**, and **Execute SQL file…** to generate the database from our exported model.

 You can also paste the following code in a query window and execute the query to achieve the same result, provided that you have created the blank database.

Reverse-engineering a database into a model

In the previous sections, we learnt how to design data models from scratch. Now that you're acquainted with the data modeling tools and diagram structures, we can move onto generating a model from an existing database.

For this part I have chosen the Sakila example database, which I introduced in *Chapter 3, Data Management with Navicat*. If you already followed the tutorials in the previous chapter, you must have a working copy of the **sakila** database available to be reverse-engineered into a data model. If not, now is a good time to take a look into it and at least follow the steps to get the **sakila** database imported into your MySQL server.

Go to Navicat's main window and locate the **sakila** database in the **connections** pane; right-click on its name and select **Reverse Database to Model…** from the pop-up menu.

A new model design window should instantly show up featuring all the tables and relationships of the Sakila database in a visual diagram, as shown in the following screenshot:

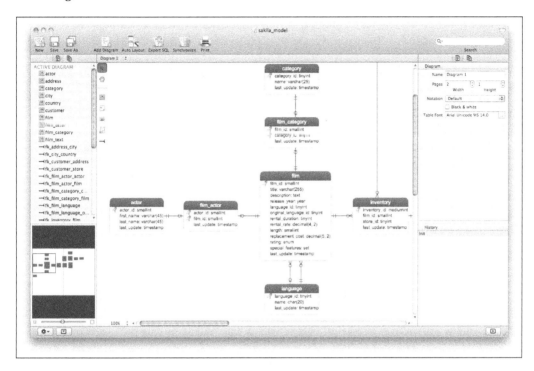

You could experiment with applying what you have learned in this chapter, for example, by adding notes and layers, and fine-tuning joining lines.

If you end up modifying the model with added tables, fields, and relationships, you can synchronize these changes back to the **sakila** database without having to regenerate the entire database from a SQL file.

To do this, simply hit the **Synchronize** button on the toolbar (on the Mac) or select **Tools | Synchronize to Database...** from the menu bar (on Windows).

Details on the data synchronization process and its settings were covered in detail in *Chapter 3, Data Management with Navicat.*

Summary

We started the chapter by getting you acquainted with the visual data modeler of Navicat, the metaphors it introduces, and how to design tables, fields, constraints, and relationships between these objects. These are both visual and form-based tools, which resemble other tools of Navicat covered in the previous chapters.

Using these tools, you learned how to design a database model from scratch and then actually generated that database from the model.

Finally, we reverse-engineered a larger, existing database and automatically generated its visual model with a one-click wizard, and you have learned how you can synchronize your changes back to the database as you progress on the model.

5
Database Maintenance and Security Management

MySQL is one of the most popular database platforms, very widely used for powering database-driven websites on the Internet and often used by web applications programmed in PHP. MySQL offers features, such as high performance, ease-of-use, and easy installation, yet a very efficient security mechanism. However, prior to Version 5.5, the fact that the default installation of MySQL came with a user named **root** with no password, presents a rather worrying security vulnerability.

While MySQL 5.5 and later versions require some basic configuration that includes certain security measures with no limitation to setting a password for the **root** user right after installation, a preliminary action must be taken after a fresh installation of MySQL 5.1, by setting a password for the **root** user as early as possible. Navicat does not only make it very easy to make such configurations easy to manage, but it also provides a few useful tools for security management and database maintenance.

This chapter focuses on basic **database administrator** (**DBA**) functions regarding the security and maintenance of MySQL using Navicat. By the end of this chapter, you should be able to master how to do the following in Navicat, for MySQL:

- Create and edit MySQL users
- Manage user privileges
- Perform maintenance tasks, such as database analysis, optimization, and repairs

User and privilege management with Navicat

The first topic in MySQL database security is user and privilege management. The second button on the toolbar with icons in Navicat's main window is the **User** button. Activating it will display a list of users in the object pane. All the users that belong to the selected MySQL server in the connections pane are on the left-hand side of the screen.

Adding, editing, duplicating, and deleting users is the same as managing any other database object in Navicat, so have a quick look back if you find yourself lost. The following screenshot shows all the users that belong to the selected MySQL server:

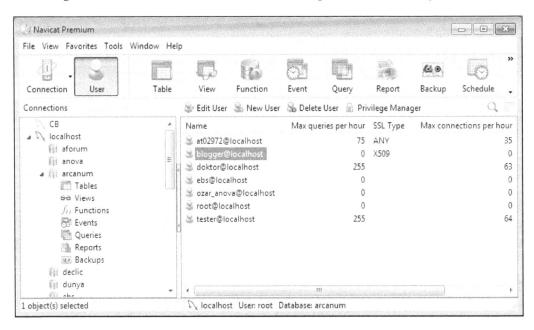

The secondary toolbar related to the user management context, in the Windows version of Navicat, explicitly showcases the utility buttons for editing an existing user, adding a new one, and deleting an existing one, besides which you will also notice a different button with a lock icon titled **Privilege Manager**. The **Privilege Manager** button was introduced in Navicat as of Version 10, and it is like a command central, where you can manage all users for all schemas, and a matrix of all privileges for an entire server, or for specific catalogs (databases) from within a single window.

On the Mac version of Navicat, the interface is quite different as there's no secondary toolbar under the main one; instead, you can use the small icons (with plus, minus, and pencil-shaped icons) at the bottom side of the window to create, edit, and delete users. As for the **Privilege Manager** button, you need to select the command **Set Privileges...** from either the **Connection** menu (when a server is selected in the connections pane) or the **Database** menu (which replaces the **Connection** menu when a database under a server is selected) from the menu bar. The following screenshot shows the list of users in the Mac platform:

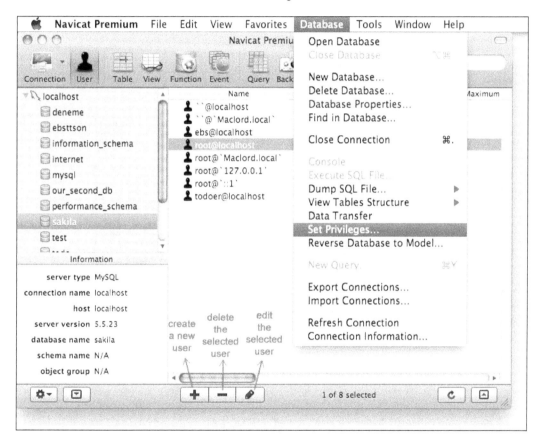

The **Privilege Manager** button gives an under-the-hood view of all the connections to the defined servers, all the databases that they have, and all kinds of privileges that are defined and set for all of the users that exist in them.

It might seem a bit complicated at first, as it is meant to control everything related to a privilege from one place. However, it is not necessarily the only means for managing the privileges. In the later section, you will see how to set them up step by step for a given user. In fact, the **Privilege Manager** button capitulates in a single interface what you will see about editing object privileges in the later section.

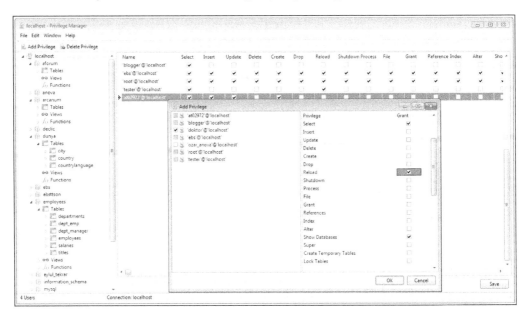

In *Chapter 1, Getting Started*, when setting up your first connection to a MySQL server, you also defined the settings for the **root** user. The root user is always listed in the object pane when you switch to the **User** view (unless deleted for a specific reason of course, and which should be a good one, I might add). An @ symbol is added as a suffix to the username, which is proceeded by the name of the server that the user is permitted to connect from; in this case, the server name is localhost. If you want the **root** user to connect from remote machines, then you must add another user with the same name; in this case the username is **root**, but specify the domain name or the IP address of that remote machine in the field labeled **Host Name**. For example, you could see myuser@workpc.

How MySQL deals with access privileges

The following pieces of information are supplied in Navicat's online manual for MySQL:

- The primary function of the MySQL privilege system is to authenticate a user that connects from a given host and to associate that user with privileges on a database, such as SELECT, INSERT, UPDATE, and DELETE.

- Information about user privileges is stored in the **user**, **db**, **host**, **tables_priv**, **columns_priv**, and **procs_priv** tables in the database named **mysql**. The MySQL server reads the contents of these tables when it starts.

- MySQL access control involves two stages when you run a client program that connects to the server, in this case Navicat:

    ◦ Stage 1: The server checks whether it should allow you to connect.

    ◦ Stage 2: Assuming that you can connect, the server checks each statement you issue to determine whether you have sufficient privileges to perform it. For example, the Create table privilege, the Drop table privilege, or the Alter table privilege.

- The server uses the **user**, **db**, and **host** tables in the **mysql** database at both stages of access control.

Diving deep into creating and editing a user in Navicat

Navicat's user designer provides the flexibility to grant or revoke server privileges to and from any user, as well as adopting a selective approach, so as to manage privileges individually on specific databases, tables, views (even individual fields), functions, and procedures.

As with any other object, in order to create and edit a user in Navicat, you can use the related toolbar buttons (described in the previous section) or right-click on the user list to select the necessary action, **Add User**, **Edit User**, or **Delete User**, from a pop-up menu.

In the user editor window that opens, it's perhaps needless to say that you have to fill in the basic user properties like the **User Name**, **Host**, and **Password** under the **General** tab.

When done, you can switch to the **Advanced** tab, where you can specify the number (limit) of queries and connections allocated to the user per hour. All the values are set to **0(default)**, which in this case means unlimited.

You want to check the **Use OLD_PASSWORD encryption** option to set passwords for any pre-4.1 clients for MySQL that need to connect to the MySQL server(s) of Version 4.1 or later. Otherwise, the server will generate long password hashes. The option does not affect authentication (MySQL 4.1 and later can still use accounts that have long password hashes), but it does prevent creation of a long password hash in the user table as the result of a password-changing operation. The following is the screenshot of the **Advanced** tab:

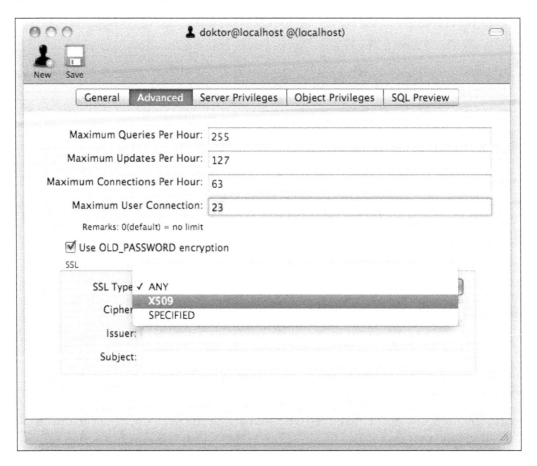

The SSL pane lets you specify SSL-related options, such as the authentication type and the certificate attributes. For more information on configuring SSL options, you can refer to the online manual of Navicat. The related section is under **Server Security Management | MySQL Security Management | MySQL User Designer | Setting Advanced MySQL Properties**.

The **Server Privileges** tab is where you can grant server-wide privileges to the user, who then applies to all the databases on that server. Once granted, the user will have the same defined permissions on all of the databases on the server. As the privileges list is in alphabetical order, all you need to do is to check or uncheck the tiny box corresponding to the list item in the second column. When you edit the **root** user, you will notice that all the privileges will appear as checked. To select (or unselect) all items from the list, right-click anywhere on the list where a pop-up menu presents the **Grant All** and **Revoke All** commands.

In Mac, under the **Object Privileges** tab, you can add individual privileges for any selected database object, be it the entire database itself, or a specific table, field, view, or procedure, as shown in the following screenshot:

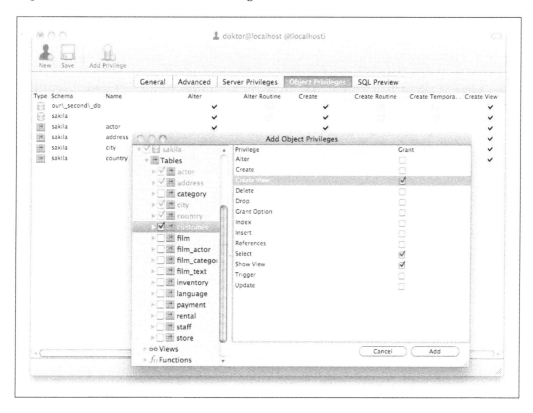

In Windows, click on the **Privileges** tab to add privileges.

To edit the specific object privileges of the user, click on **Add Privilege** to open a secondary model window, and follow these steps:

1. Expand the node(s) in the tree view displaying a hierarchy starting from the databases to the individual objects, such as tables and fields, until you reach the target object on which you want to define the privilege.

2. Check the object to show the privilege list on the right-hand pane.

3. On the list, check the **Grant** option against the permission type listed under the **Privilege** column to assign it to the user. Multiple privileges can be granted, of course.

4. Click the **Add** button when you're done, and then remember to press the **Save** button (indicated with a floppy disk icon on the main toolbar of the user editor window).

The **SQL Preview** tab generates the SQL commands, which need to be run on the server to grant or revoke the privileges, since last time that the permission settings were saved. So, these SQL commands are executed automatically after the **Save** button is hit.

Here's some example of SQL commands generated by editing the privileges:

```
GRANT Alter, Create View, Grant Option, Create ON `sakila`.* TO
`producer`@`localhost`;

GRANT Alter, Create View, Grant Option, Create ON TABLE `sakila`.`actor`
TO `producer`@`localhost`;

GRANT Alter, Create View, Grant Option, Create ON TABLE
`sakila`.`address` TO `producer`@`localhost`;

GRANT Alter, Create View, Grant Option, Create ON TABLE `sakila`.`city`
TO `producer`@`localhost`;

GRANT Alter, Create View, Grant Option, Create ON TABLE
`sakila`.`country` TO `producer`@`localhost`;

GRANT Create View, Select, Show View ON TABLE `sakila`.`customer` TO
`producer`@`localhost`;
```

Performing maintenance tasks with Navicat

Navicat provides a set of graphical tools for database and table maintenance tasks, which are in fact native MySQL services. Toward this end, Navicat supports four major tasks, which can be performed on MySQL database tables:

- Analysis
- Check
- Optimization
- Repairs

When this book was being authored, Navicat did not have a special menu (in the menu bar) or a button for triggering these tasks. Basically, you need to have switched to **Table** or **View** in Navicat's main window and right-clicked on a table or view on which you want to perform one of these tasks. Then, from the pop-up menu select **Maintain**, and then select the related task as the sub-menu item. Now, let's take a closer look at what these tasks are and what they are good for, as shown in the following screenshot:

Analyzing a MySQL table or view with Navicat

The **Analyze Table** command analyzes and stores the key distribution for the selected table. MySQL uses the stored key distribution to decide in which order the tables should be joined.

When an analysis is started, the table is locked with a read lock if the table has MyISAM or BDB as the underlying database engine. In the case of InnoDB, the table is locked with a write lock. Currently, MySQL supports analysis only for MyISAM, BDB, and InnoDB tables. For MyISAM tables, this action is the equivalent of running the command `myisamchk --analyze`.

Checking a table or view

This maintenance task checks a table for errors. When this book was being written, MySQL supported the checking of only MyISAM, InnoDB, and ARCHIVE tables. When MyISAM tables are checked, their key statistics are also updated.

Additional options for checking are summarized in the table below:

Options	Functions
Quick	Does not scan the rows to check for incorrect links. This applies to InnoDB and MyISAM tables and views.
Fast	Checks only those tables that have not been closed properly. This applies only to MyISAM tables and views.
Changed	Checks only those tables that have been changed since the last check or that have not been closed properly. This applies only to MyISAM tables and views.
Extended	Does a full key lookup for all the keys for each row. This ensures that the table is 100 percent consistent, but takes a long time. It applies only to MyISAM tables and views.

Optimization made easy

The main reason for optimizing your table is to reclaim unused space and defragment the datafile associated with the table. You should optimize a table if you have deleted a considerable number of rows from that table or frequently updated a table with variable-length rows (tables with `varchar`, `blob`, or `text` fields). Thanks to the task of optimization, deleted records are maintained in a linked list, and subsequent `INSERT` operations reuse old row positions.

MySQL supported optimization only for MyISAM, InnoDB, and BDB tables when this book was being written.

For MyISAM tables, table optimization works as follows:

- If the table has deleted or split rows, repair the table
- If the index pages are not sorted, sort them
- If the table's statistics are not up-to-date (and the repair could not be accomplished by sorting the index), update them

Repairing a table

The title means what it says. If you suspect a table is corrupt or just not exactly in good working order, you can do **Repair Table**, and it just solves all of the problems in most cases. Repairs can be performed in two modes — **Quick** or **Extended**. A **Quick** repair only attempts to fix the index tree of a table. In the extended mode, MySQL creates the index row by row, instead of creating one index at a time.

Summary

You have just made it to the end of this chapter. By now, you should be able to create, edit, and delete users in Navicat, assign them server-wide privileges, and even define individual privileges for specific database objects and assign them for a given user.

When it comes to troubleshooting, you also now know what it takes to analyze and check what the error is with a MySQL table or view, and to make sure they are running okay. You also learned how to optimize and repair a MySQL table with Navicat's one-click maintenance tool.

6
Designing Reports with Navicat

A powerful **Report Builder** came with the Windows version of Navicat Version 10, and exclusively in its Enterprise Edition, when this book was being written. With Navicat's Report Builder, you can present data from your MySQL databases in various reports, such as invoices, sales figures, order summaries, even forms, and mailing labels (also known as mail merge). You can even set a scheduler (see *Chapter 3, Data Management with Navicat*) to have the reports automatically delivered at a specific time and/or at defined intervals.

As you will see in the next sections, the look and feel of Navicat's **Report Designer** resembles the **Report Module** of Microsoft Access in many ways.

To be able to follow the tutorial in this chapter, you need to have imported the Sakila example database introduced in *Chapter 3, Data Management with Navicat*.

As of Version 10 of Navicat Premium and Navicat for MySQL, a powerful Report Builder tool is included in the Enterprise Edition for Windows. This chapter will train you to develop skills, such as:

- Preparing a dataset by designing queries for reports in a GUI
- Designing reports using a wizard
- Customizing the report design
- Printing to a paper or file in a variety of formats

First contact with the tool(s)

In order to access Navicat's **Report Manager**, all you need to do is to select the server and the database from the left navigation pane, and then click on the big **Report** button from the toolbar of Navicat's main window. Alternatively, you may select **View | Report** from the main menu bar. Once in the context of **Report** (Manager), you can use the buttons on the secondary toolbar to create, edit, or delete reports, or right-click anywhere in the object pane to invoke a pop-up menu that will let you perform the same actions, as shown in the following screenshot:

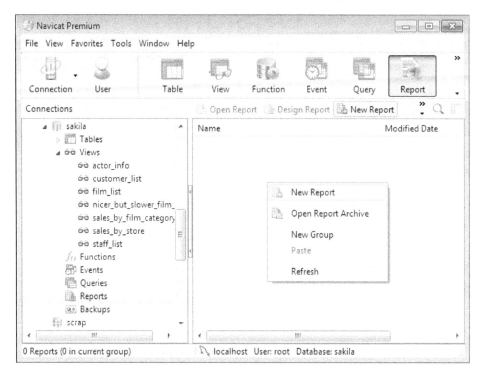

Now let's go ahead and design a simple report based on the view named **film_list** from the **sakila** database.

Create a new report using one of the previously described methods. A new, larger **Untitled** window should appear, with its **Design** tab active by default. You will also notice that the user interface of this window is probably the most complex among all the other tools that Navicat features, as Navicat's Report Designer is a full-blown report-building application as it is.

What we need to do first with a blank report is to select a dataset with which we will populate our report. Therefore, we need to switch to the **Data** tab of this window to specify the source of the report's data.

Preparing the data with Query Wizard

The **Data** tab presents us with a blank page when opening it for the first time. It is very difficult to figure out what the next step will be from here. Refer to the following screenshot:

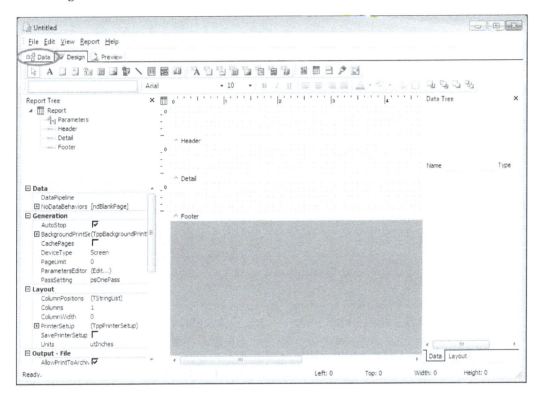

To specify some data source at this point is a little frustrating, as right-clicking on the empty area yields nothing, and there's no toolbar under the **Data** tab either. Rather, you need to go to the **File** menu of the menu bar and select **New…**. This will bring up a small, modal dialog box asking you to run **Query Wizard** or **Query Designer**, as shown in the following screenshot:

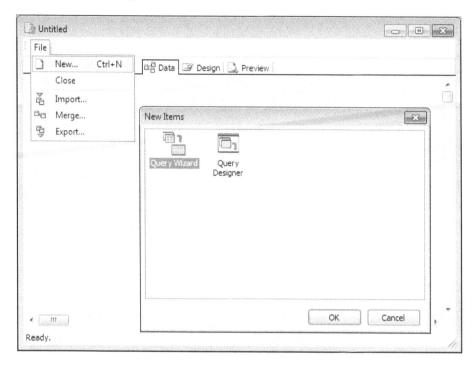

We'll go with **Query Wizard** at this time, so make sure that its icon is highlighted, and then click on **OK**. The **Query Wizard** window displays two, scrollable listboxes (side by side) that some programmers also call shuttle lists. The list box on the left-hand side titled **Available Tables** contains the names of all **Tables** and **Views** from our **sakila** database, and the one on the right-hand side titled **Selected Tables** indicates the items we have picked from the available ones.

You will have to click and select one or more items from the list on the left, which will be transferred to the list on the right as soon as you press the **>** button.

For the sake of our simple tutorial, we only need the **film_list** view. Just select it by clicking on its name and move it to the list box titled **Selected Tables**, and then click on **Next**. The screenshot of the **Query Wizard** window is as follows:

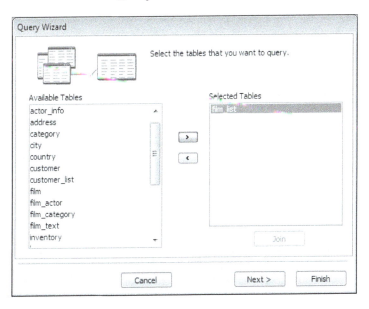

You can skip the next screen simply by clicking on **Next** again, since we want all the fields from the database view we have chosen, and this option is already selected in this screen by default.

In the screen displaying if we want to **Add calculated fields to the query**, we will skip it again by clicking on **No Calculations** and clicking on **Next** one more time.

Now we are presented with the option of **Group rows together based on common field values**, which we also want to pass by clicking on **No Grouping** and clicking on **Next** once more.

As for the **Limit the rows returned** screen, we want no limit here, so leave **All rows** selected without changing anything else, and hit **Next** again. After clicking on **Next**, the window displayed will look similar to the following screenshot:

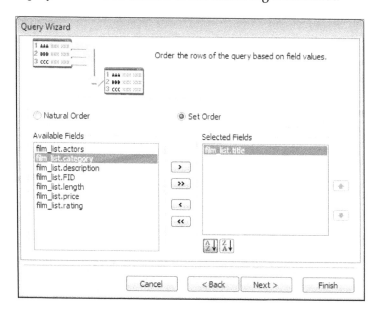

Here, we will be asked about the way the rows of the dataset we selected will be ordered. The default option is **Natural Order**, which should bring the results to the report in the same order as they would appear in the **View** (which would most probably sort the items by ID). However, I think it would be a good idea to sort them by both category and film title for our report. So select **Set Order** and then move **film_list.category** to the list box titled **Selected Fields**, and then do the same for the **film_list.title**, and finally click on **Next** for the last time.

The last step will ask us to give our query a name of our choice, and before we finally click on **Finish**, we can indicate our preference of whether to **Return to the data workspace**, **Preview the query**, or **Modify the query's design**. Go with the first option, which is the default anyway. So when we're done, our data workspace will now contain the **film_list** view, as shown in the following screenshot:

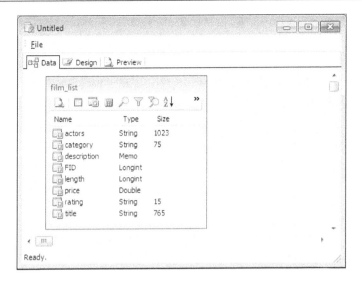

Now to get an idea of the dataset we just prepared, click on the first tiny button on the toolbar of the **film_list** window, which will bring up a pop-up window titled **Preview Data – film_list** displaying the film records from the query that we just created. You might need to enlarge the window and manually adjust the column lengths by hovering the mouse arrow over the column heading borders and then clicking-and-dragging the columns to the desired length, as shown in the following screenshot:

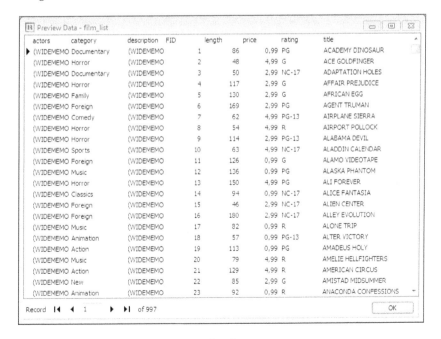

When you are done with previewing the query results, just click on **OK** at the bottom-right of this window.

The other seven buttons on the toolbar help us open up the **Query Designer** window for reports, and this window lets you modify the query by selecting the tables and fields, defining the filtering criteria, grouping the fields, and so on.

Now, you can click on the second button on the toolbar of the **film_list** table to invoke the **Query Designer** with its **Tables** tab active, to add more tables or views to the query by joining them. Similarly, the third button will help you open **Query Designer** with its **Fields** tab active, to modify the selected fields, which we specified using the **Query Wizard** in the first place, as shown in the following screenshot:

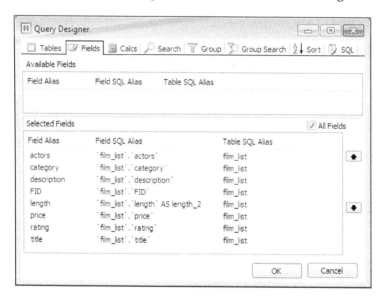

Query Designer has some advanced features, which will only be mentioned here briefly, but not be covered in detail.

The **Calcs** tab, for example, is where you can define some dynamic fields with aggregate functions, such as sum(), avg(), min(), max(), and count(), or any SQL expression you can use as a function that MySQL supports.

Another example is the **Search** tab, in which you can define some pre-filtering criteria, and which will be added to the SQL query as a WHERE condition.

For the sake of this simple report, we will leave the **Query Designer** for now, and switch to the **Design** tab of the Report Builder to finally start working on our report's layout. When we go back to the **Design** tab, we are reminded that the canvas that was divided into three areas, as **Header**, **Detail**, and **Footer** (also as indicated in the upper left pane titled **Report Tree)**, is still blank. However, on the right-hand side of the window, we now see **film_list** under **Data Tree** and **Fields for film_list** below it.

Designing the report

While it is possible for us to design our report's layout by clicking-and-dragging the fields listed from the right-hand side onto the canvas and aligning them as desired, this is how a report is normally designed without wizards. This can get quite complex, so I will show you an easier way, which will help finish this report in no time.

Go to the **File** menu and select **New…**. A new dialog box titled **New Items** will pop up and will present us with four buttons as icons labeled **Report Wizard**, **Report**, **Label Templates**, and **Cross Tab Wizard** respectively. I promised the easier way, so we want the **Report Wizard** for this. It should be highlighted by default, but make sure it's selected. Then click on **OK**, as shown in the following screenshot:

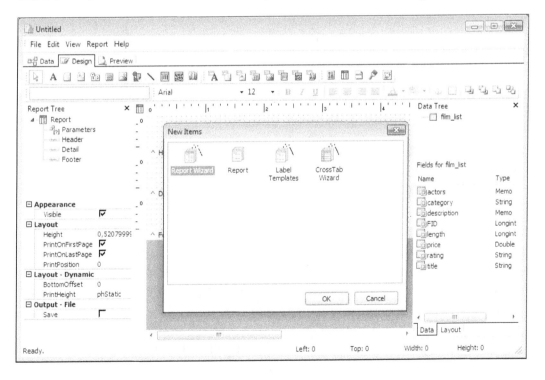

Now, we should see a modal window titled **Report Wizard**, which is very similar to the wizards in other applications, such as Microsoft Access. The usage of this wizard is quite intuitive as each step includes understandable explanations and user interface elements. On the first screen of **Report Wizard**, you will be asked to select the dataset and its fields, which you require to appear on the report.

For this report, add **FID**, **title**, **category**, **actors**, **rating**, and **price** to the selected fields in this very order, and then click on **Next**.

The next screen of **Report Wizard** is where we can specify groups in which the selected data might be categorized. Click on **category** from **Available Fields** and move it to the **Groups** list box by pressing the corresponding down arrow located between the two list boxes. When you do that, you should also note that the report layout preview would be updated by reflecting this change, as shown in the following screenshot:

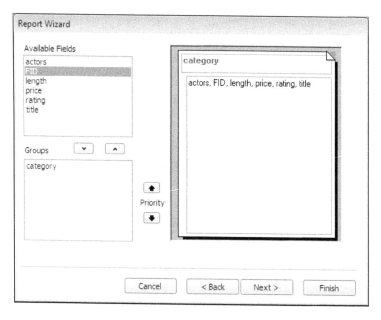

Click on **Next** to proceed to the screen, where we will pick a **Layout** style and choose the (default) page printing **Orientation**. Now because we have opted to group the report output according to category, we are presented with a total of six **Layout** style options here. In the other case, we would have had only two layouts to choose from—**Vertical** (print labels or cards style) or plain **Tabular**.

The **Layout** style options that we have, in this case, are:

- **Stepped**
- **Block**
- **Outline 1**
- **Outline 2**
- **Align Left 1**
- **Align Left 2**

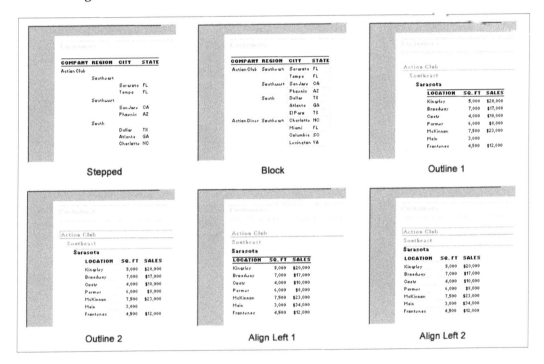

As for the **Orientation** options, they simply consist of **Portrait** and **Landscape**, with which you should be exceedingly familiar from the printing options in other programs that you use every day.

For our report, I will urge you to choose **Align Left 2** as the **Layout** style and the page (printing) **Orientation** option as **Portrait**, which is the default. And unless you are eager to later have the hassle of adjusting the column widths on the report layout manually, you should leave the option **Adjust field widths so all fields fit on page** checked.

Click on **Next** when you're done here. Refer to the following screenshot:

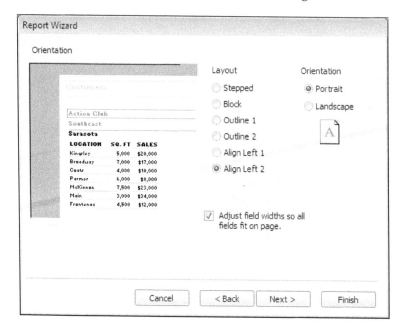

The **Report Wizard** window will ask you to pick a thematic style from a choice list of ready-made report designs or templates, for which you have the following options:

- **Bold**
- **Casual**
- **Compact**
- **Corporate**
- **Formal**
- **Soft Gray**

Although, in a left-hand side design preview when each option is clicked, it is dynamically updated to give you an idea about what your report will look like. It might be a good idea to experiment with this as many times as you can, so that you can get familiar with each style reflected on your reports.

My personal favorite here is **Casual**, which you will see in the screenshots of the report designs and previews from this point on in the chapter.

When you click on **Next**, you will be thankful that all the necessary information to create the report has been provided by now, and you will be presented with the choices of previewing your report right away or heading straight to modifying the report's design.

First, let's do some final retouches before we preview the report, so check the second option before you click on **Finish**.

As we get back to the Report Design, we will happily notice that the canvas is no longer blank. Also, **Title**, **Header**, **Detail**, and **Footer** are a bit weird, as they are all filled in with the labels and data placeholders that we defined in **Report Wizard** earlier, but still appear to be small.

In order to make the report look more "human", we can start by changing the title to something more natural such as `Sakila Movie List`, and modify the column header labels by giving them nicer names. For example, name it `Item #` instead of **FID** (which stands for film ID). Refer to the following screenshot:

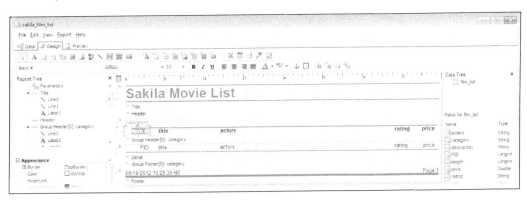

You will also want to resize column widths to use the space efficiently. For example, you will especially notice that the **rating**, **price**, and **category** columns are unnecessarily wider than they should be. So, you can move them towards the right and reduce their width. Then, increase the width for **actors** and **title**. Remember to vertically align the column name and the data field (the placeholder for data), which are placed in the header and detail areas respectively.

Also, tweaking the appearance of the **category** field is highly recommended, which will substantially affect the look and feel of the report, so as to make it appear more pleasing to the eye.

Switching to the Preview tab

Now, it's about time we switched to the **Preview** tab to see what our report and its output looks like.

In the report preview, you can experiment with the buttons on the toolbar to adjust your viewing settings, such as choosing how to fit the report data to the page, printing options, as well as text search on the report's output. You can also navigate between the pages of the report using the tiny, arrow-shaped buttons. Refer to the following screenshot:

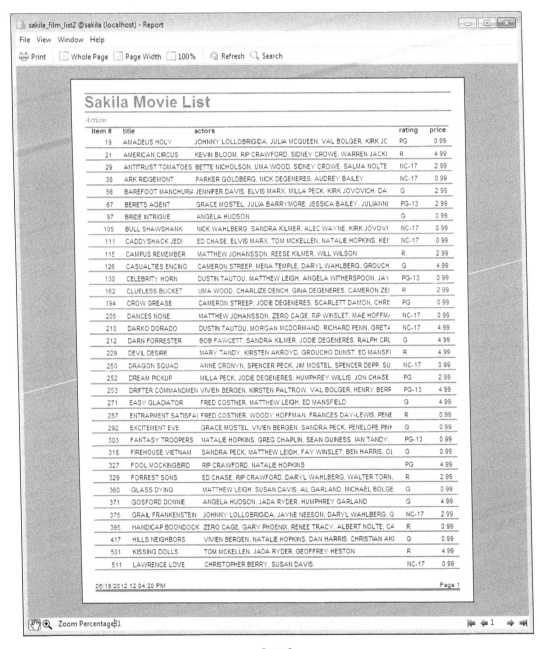

Now is a good time to save the report if you haven't already done so. Navicat has some specificity in saving reports, unlike how it treats other objects, such as **Queries**, **Events**, and **Models**. First of all, to save your report you need to go to the menu bar and choose **File | Save**. When you're saving the report for the first time, you will be prompted with a standard **Save As** dialog box. Then, specify a name for the report that will be suffixed with the file extension .rtm and a location in the filesystem, which suggests that you can store your reports anywhere on your drive. However, as soon as you click on the **Save** button of the dialog box, Navicat will prompt you with a confirmation alert warning you that if you save your report outside Navicat's default directory for reports, your report will not be visible in the **Reports** view within the program (in which case you will have to locate the report using an **Open File** dialog box every time you need to access it in Navicat). Refer to the following screenshot:

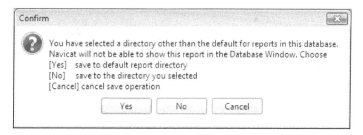

Even if you would like to have the report file in a specific folder in the file, it is probably a good idea to save to the default location, which you can access in Windows Explorer by going through the following path:

\Users\<user_name>\Documents\Navicat\MySQL\servers\localhost\sakila

After you save your report and exit **Report Designer**, you will need to right-click on its name in the **Report** view and select **Design Report** from the pop-up menu. Double-clicking on a saved report directly brings the report output window, (which is very similar to the **Preview** tab of the designer) from which you can print the report or just view its contents as it is on the screen.

You can not only print your reports on paper, but also produce output in a variety of formats including PDF, Excel, text, and HTML. You can specify this option, on the fly, in the **Print** dialog box.

If you are aiming at a text-based output, you may want to tweak some more settings by selecting **File | Print to File Setup...** and specifying some parameters, such as column delimiters and the fields to include in the output.

Navicat's report building and management can do more than what's discussed in this chapter and than what is outside the scope of this introductory book. But you can explore these features in depth, by experimenting yourself and also by referring to Navicat's own manual accessible from its website. There you can also find more step-by-step and screen-by-screen tutorials, which could teach you how to create more advanced reports, such as invoices, detailed order summaries, sales statistics, crosstab reports, mailing labels, and even photo albums.

Summary

Building a report in Navicat consists of two major phases—preparing the data and designing the report based on that data.

In this chapter, we have seen the report building and management tools of Navicat, and the basics of designing reports by following a simple tutorial, which also helps in getting acquainted with some of the tools that can be used for more advanced purposes.

We have also seen how the reports can be printed on a paper as well as exported to a variety of popular file formats.

Additional Tips and Tricks

Throughout this book, we've covered some of the most useful and most common tasks in Navicat, but not everything it has to offer. This appendix aims at giving you some additional tips and tricks about using some of the not-so-obvious features of Navicat, such as:

- Copying your settings to another Navicat user or computer
- Monitoring the MySQL server and intervening the running processes
- Power searching databases and discovering a new way of designing queries

Transferring your settings from one computer to another

In cases where you work with more than one computer (where each computer has a copy of Navicat), you might want to have your settings, connection profiles, custom queries, data model diagrams, and even batch jobs copied across all the computers you use. Even if this is not the case, you can use the tips here to back up your Navicat settings for restoring the data later, in the event of resetting up your computer.

Transferring settings on the Mac

All of your settings, connection profiles, saved queries, and models in Navicat are stored in two folders on the Mac, which reside in `/Users/<user_name>/Library/ Application Support/`. You can customize the **Data Models Path** from the **Preferences** window (simply select **Preferences…** from the application menu next to the **Apple** menu, and go to the **File Paths** tab in the opening window). One of the folders under `Application Support` is named `PremiumSoft CyberTech`, and the other is `Navicat Premium` or `Navicat for MySQL`, depending on the edition and version you're using.

In Finder, select **Go | Go to Folder...** from the menu bar (or just press the **+** and **G** keys simultaneously) and type /Users/<user_name>/Library/Application Support/, and then press the **Go** button to get there. And finally, copy these two folders to the same folder hierarchy on the target machine or the user.

This will copy all of your settings, connection profiles, and saved model diagrams to the target machine. The target machine or the user should not be running Navicat while this transfer is in progress. Refer to the following screenshot:

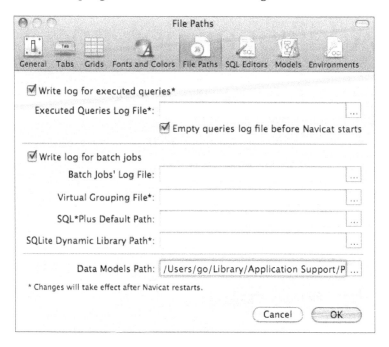

Transferring settings on Windows

Certain user data, such as queries and data model diagrams, as well as reports (exclusive to the Windows version) of Navicat are stored inside the Navicat directory, by default, in the user's Documents folder. Other settings and connection profiles are stored in the registry in the Windows version.

You can export the connection settings by going through **File | Export Connections...** in Navicat's main menu bar, or right-clicking on a connection definition (database server name) from the left pane and selecting the same menu item. Then on the target system (or the user account) you can repeat the same steps, except choosing **Import Connections...** this time and specifying the previously exported file (and its path) through an **open file** dialog box.

In Windows 7, the complete pathname to the user's documents folder would be something like `C:\Users\<user_name>\Documents\Navicat`.

It is possible, however, to customize the default directory (and paths) by going to **Tools | Options | Miscellaneous**.

You can transfer the queries and data model diagrams to another Windows PC by simply copying the entire `Navicat` folder to the target user's `Documents` folder. Make sure Navicat is not running on the target machine while you perform this transfer. Refer to the following screenshot:

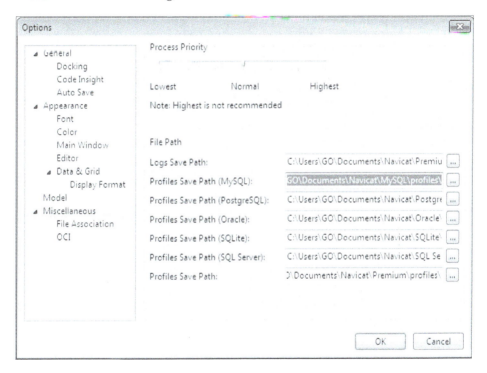

Monitoring the MySQL Server

With Navicat, you can monitor your database server(s) to view the running processes, the server's current status, as well as the properties of the databases, such as the variables. It is possible to get this information in real time for all of your servers, in a single, under-the-hood view.

Server monitor is accessible directly from the **Tools** menu in Navicat's main menu bar, and it has three main views categorized by tabs in the Windows version and main toolbar buttons in the Mac version. Refer to the following screenshot:

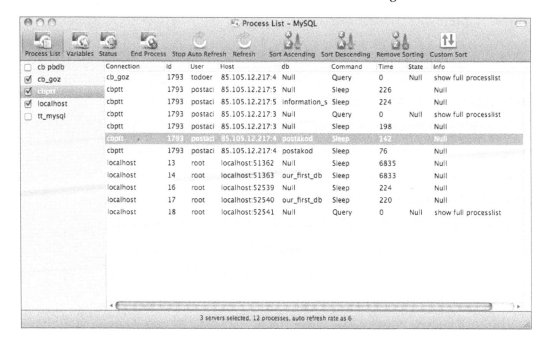

The process list

This is where you see the running processes or tasks on all servers, selected in the checkbox list on the right-hand side pane of the window. The information you get on this screen can be listed as follows:

- The server name that is defined in the connection settings
- **ID** of the process running on the server
- **User** who logged on to the server
- **Host** or the IP from which the user is connected
- The name of the database that is currently being used
- Last **Command** that was issued by the user
- **Time**, **State**, and **Info** of the process

It is possible to forcibly end a process simply by clicking on it from the list to get it highlighted and hitting the **End Process** button.

You will also notice the other buttons on the toolbar that provide you with an option of refreshing the view automatically or manually. One not-so-obvious trick is that in the case of auto-refreshing, you can change the interval of the **1** second default to whatever you prefer, by choosing **Set Refresh Rate...** from the **Edit** menu.

Variables

Under this tab, you can get all the server variables, such as **character_set_server** and **date_format**, and the values set for these variables listed in alphabetical order. This information is normally gotten by executing the **SHOW VARIABLES** command in the MySQL server console.

It is possible to change the values on the fly, simply by selecting a row and clicking the square-shaped button at the right end of the cell containing the variable value. (A feature for advanced users who really know what they're doing.)

Status

The **status** tab lists the same standard information that would otherwise be retrieved from a MySQL server by issuing the **SHOW STATUS** command.

This outputs some long, read-only information understandable by advanced users and DBAs.

Revealing a hidden search feature of Navicat

You can use Navicat to locate one or more database table records matching a certain criteria. After you select a database or schema from the left-hand side pane of Navicat's main window and right-click on it, you will see the **Find in database...** command among the items of the opening pop-up menu. Issuing this command will reveal a pop-up window that will let you enter a search string and matching criteria (such as **Exact** or **Contains**, or even evaluate a **Regular Expression**).

For example, select **our_first_db** that we created in *Chapter 2, Working with Databases*, and right-click on it and choose **Find in database...**. Then, enter manager in the search box, leave the matching criterion as **Contains**, and click on the **Find** button.

The search should yield 12 matches and the results should be summarized below the search box. What's cool about this feature is that, when you double-click on one of the results, a new query window will open up with a generated SQL query that was translated from our search criteria, which is automatically executed once, with the results displayed below it. Refer to the following screenshot:

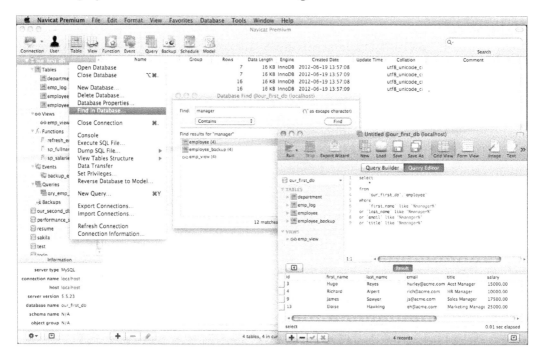

Summary

This appendix provided us with some additional tips and tricks, such as how to backup or transfer our Navicat settings. What's more? We have unraveled some more hidden features of Navicat (such as the **Server Monitor**), which not only give us detailed information about running processes, such as the client user information and command type run by the connected user, but full control to manually terminate processes as well. We also saw how to get other detailed information, such as server variables and server statuses, using this powerful tool.

Lastly, we have seen a search feature that enables us to retrieve specific records from any table containing the searched string and automatically generates a SQL query, which can be reused to perform the same search later as a standard Navicat query.

Index

P

Passphrase field 10
Password field 10
Port field 9, 10
PremiumSoft 65
Preview tab 105-108
Print dialog box 107
Private Key field 10
Privilege Manager button 82, 84
Privileges tab 87
procedures
  working with 29-32
process list 112
Properties palette 67, 68

Q

query
  building 38-41
  designing 35-38
Query button 35
Query Designer window 100
Query Wizard
  data, preparing with 95-100
Query Wizard window 96, 97
quick option 90
Quick repair 91

R

report
  designing 101-105
Report Builder 93
Report button 94
Report Designer 94
Report Manager 94
Report Module 93
Report Wizard window 102, 104
Restore Backup option 61
reverse-engineering
  database, into model 78, 79
Revoke All commands 87
root user 84
Run button 31, 37

S

sakila database
  about 44, 79
  dump file, URL for downloading 44
Save As button 18, 63
Save As dialog box 107
Save button 107
Schedule tab 34
Secure Shell. *See* SSH
Secure Sockets Layer. *See* SSL
security option 28
Server monitor 112
Server Privileges tab 87
Set Task Schedule button 63
settings
  transferring, from one computer
    to another 109
  transferring, on Mac 109, 110
  transferring, on Windows 110
show objects in connection tree option 15
SHOW STATUS command 113
SHOW VARIABLES command 113
Simple To Do database 71, 77
SQL
  model diagram, exporting 77, 78
SQL dump file
  used, for creating database schema 45-49
SQL Preview tab 21, 88
SSH 10
SSL 11
start button 46
status tab 113
structure synchronization 58, 59
synchronize button 79

T

table
  analyzing 90
  changed option 90
  checking 90
  creating 18, 19
  data, entering 24, 25

extended option 90
fast option 90
file, importing 55, 56
optimizing 91
quick option 90
repairing 91
viewing 90
Table button 16
Tables tab active 100
task table 71
Temptable algorithm 28
triggers
defining 22, 23
Triggers tab 22

U

Untitled window 94
unwanted objects
deleting 76
Use OLD_PASSWORD encryption
option 86

user
creating 85, 86
editing 85, 86
user and privilege management 82-84
user button 82
User Name field 10

V

View Builder tab 26
View Builder, visual editing tool 26
views
creating 26, 29

W

WHERE condition 100
Windows
settings, transferring on 110

Thank you for buying
MySQL Management and Administration with Navicat

About Packt Publishing

Packt, pronounced 'packed', published its first book "Mastering phpMyAdmin for Effective MySQL Management" in April 2004 and subsequently continued to specialize in publishing highly focused books on specific technologies and solutions.

Our books and publications share the experiences of your fellow IT professionals in adapting and customizing today's systems, applications, and frameworks. Our solution based books give you the knowledge and power to customize the software and technologies you're using to get the job done. Packt books are more specific and less general than the IT books you have seen in the past. Our unique business model allows us to bring you more focused information, giving you more of what you need to know, and less of what you don't.

Packt is a modern, yet unique publishing company, which focuses on producing quality, cutting-edge books for communities of developers, administrators, and newbies alike. For more information, please visit our website: www.packtpub.com.

About Packt Enterprise

In 2010, Packt launched two new brands, Packt Enterprise and Packt Open Source, in order to continue its focus on specialization. This book is part of the Packt Enterprise brand, home to books published on enterprise software – software created by major vendors, including (but not limited to) IBM, Microsoft and Oracle, often for use in other corporations. Its titles will offer information relevant to a range of users of this software, including administrators, developers, architects, and end users.

Writing for Packt

We welcome all inquiries from people who are interested in authoring. Book proposals should be sent to author@packtpub.com. If your book idea is still at an early stage and you would like to discuss it first before writing a formal book proposal, contact us; one of our commissioning editors will get in touch with you.

We're not just looking for published authors; if you have strong technical skills but no writing experience, our experienced editors can help you develop a writing career, or simply get some additional reward for your expertise.

MySQL Admin Cookbook

ISBN: 978-1-847197-96-2   Paperback: 376 pages

99 great recipes for mastering MySQL configuration and administration

1. Set up MySQL to perform administrative tasks such as efficiently managing data and database schema, improving the performance of MySQL servers, and managing user credentials

2. Deal with typical performance bottlenecks and lock-contention problems

3. Restrict access sensibly and regain access to your database in case of loss of administrative user credentials

Mastering phpMyAdmin 3.4 for Effective MySQL Management

ISBN: 978-1-849517-78-2   Paperback: 394 pages

A complete guide to getting started with phpMyAdmin 3.4 and mastering its features

1. A step-by-step tutorial for manipulating data with the latest version of phpmyadmin

2. Administer your MySQL databases with phpMyAdmin

3. Manage users and privileges with MySQL Server Administration tools

Please check **www.PacktPub.com** for information on our titles

MySQL 5.1 Plugin Development

ISBN: 978-1-849510-60-8   Paperback: 288 pages

Extend MySQL to suit your needs with this unique guide into the world of MySQL plugins

1. A practical guide with working examples explained line by line

2. Add new functions to MySQL with User Defined Functions

3. Export information via SQL using the INFORMATION_SCHEMA plugins

High Availability MySQL Cookbook

ISBN: 978-1-847199-94-2   Paperback: 264 pages

Over 50 simple but incredibly effective recipes focusing on different methods of achieving high availability for MySQL databases

1. Analyze and learn different high availability options, including clustering and replication solutions within MySQL

2. Improve uptime of your MySQL databases with simple recipes showing powerful high availability techniques for MySQL

3. Tune your MySQL database for optimal performance.

Please check **www.PacktPub.com** for information on our titles

www.ingramcontent.com/pod-product-compliance
Lightning Source LLC
LaVergne TN
LVHW080059070326
832902LV00014B/2320